Chronicles

Chronicles

On Our Troubled Times

THOMAS PIKETTY

Translated from the French and annotated by
Seth Ackerman

VIKING
an imprint of
PENGUIN BOOKS

VIKING

UK | USA | Canada | Ireland | Australia
India | New Zealand | South Africa

Viking is part of the Penguin Random House group of companies
whose addresses can be found at global.penguinrandomhouse.com.

This collection first published in the United States of America by
Houghton Mifflin Harcourt as *Why Save the Bankers?* 2016
First published in Great Britain by Viking as *Chronicles* 2016
001

Portions of this book were previously published in *Peut-on sauver l'Europe?* and
will be published in *Chroniques 2012–2016*

Set in 12/14.75 pt Bembo Book MT Std
Typeset by Jouve (UK), Milton Keynes
Printed in Great Britain by Clays Ltd, St Ives plc

A CIP catalogue record for this book is available from the British Library

Hardback ISBN: 978–0–241–23489–1
Trade Paperback ISBN: 978–0–241–23491–4

www.greenpenguin.co.uk

Penguin Random House is committed to a
sustainable future for our business, our readers
and our planet. This book is made from Forest
Stewardship Council® certified paper.

Contents

Contents

Translator's Note

I have translated these essays as they originally appeared in the pages of the French newspapers *Libération* and, in one case, *Le Monde*. Since they often refer to people and events that would have been familiar to a French newspaper reader, but not necessarily to readers of this book, I have added explanatory notes, situating them in the context of their time, and defining some French references.

Because many of these essays discuss the Eurozone crisis and assume a working knowledge of the functioning of the European Union, it may be useful to sketch a few relevant facts. The EU's executive branch is composed of two decision-making bodies. The European Council, or Council of Heads of State, brings together national leaders at regular closed-door summits focused on setting broad policy priorities and resolving high-level disagreements. The Council of the European Union is made up of national ministers who meet regularly to set policy in specific areas. Those bodies work together with the appointed European Commission, an elite executive institution that administers policy and proposes legislation, often on the urging of the European Council. Legislation generally must be approved by both the European Council and the directly elected European Parliament. The EU's ensemble of institutions also includes judicial and monetary authorities: the European Court of Justice and the European Central Bank, or ECB.

During the period in which these essays were written,

Croatia's integration into the EU brought the total number of member states to twenty-eight. When the first articles in this book were published, seventeen of those states shared the euro as their common currency; at the time of this writing, that number stood at nineteen. This group of EU states, collectively called the Eurozone, is expected to expand further – provided the euro survives.

Preface

This book brings together many of my published monthly newspaper columns, with no subsequent updating or revision. Some of these pieces have aged a bit, others less so. Taken together, they represent one social scientist's effort to understand and analyze the day-to-day world, to get involved in the public debate; an attempt to reconcile the rigors and responsibilities of scholarship with those of citizenship.

The years during which these columns were written were deeply marked by the world financial crisis that began in 2007–8 and is still ongoing. On several occasions, I tried to understand the new role of central banks as they sought to avert a collapse of the world economy, or to analyze the similarities and differences between the Irish and Greek crises. Not to mention traditional domestic topics, still vital for our common future. But toward the end of the period, one question began to eclipse all the others: Will the European Union be able to live up to the hopes that so many of us have placed in it? Will Europe manage to become the continental power, and the space for democratic sovereignty, that we'll need in order to take control of a globalized capitalism gone mad? Or will it once again be no more than a technocratic instrument of deregulation, intensified competition, and the subjection of governments to the markets?

At first glance, the financial crisis that began in the summer of 2007 with the collapse of the U.S. subprime mortgage market and the September 2008 bankruptcy of Lehman

Brothers can be seen as the first crisis of twenty-first-century globalized patrimonial capitalism.

Let's review. Starting in the 1980s, a new wave of financial deregulation and an outsized faith in self-regulating markets descended on the world. The memory of the Great Depression of the 1930s and the cataclysms that followed had faded. The 'stagflation' of the 1970s (a mixture of economic stagnation and inflation) had showed the limits of the Keynesian consensus of the 1950s and '60s, hastily constructed in the specific context of the postwar decades.* Naturally, with postwar reconstruction and high growth rates coming to an end, the continual growth of taxes and expansion of government that characterized the 1950s and '60s could no longer be taken for granted.† The deregulation movement began in 1979–80 in the United States and United Kingdom, where there was rising unease as the economies of Japan, Germany, and France caught up with – and, in the British case, surpassed – their own. Riding the wave of discontent, Ronald Reagan and Margaret Thatcher explained that government was the problem, not the solution. They called for escaping a welfare state that had made entrepreneurs soft, a return to the pure capitalism of the pre-World War I era. The process accelerated and then spread to continental Europe after 1990–91. The fall of the Soviet Union left capitalism without a rival, and a new era began in which many chose to believe in an 'end of history' and a 'new economy' based on permanent stock market euphoria.

---

* Referred to in France as the Trente Glorieuses, the 'thirty glorious' years from 1945 to 1975. – *Trans.*

† In France, the real growth rate of national income fell from an average of 5.2 percent per year between 1949 and 1979 to 1.7 percent between 1979 and 2009 – a two-thirds reduction.

In the early 2000s, stock market and real estate values in Europe and the United States matched and then surpassed their previous peaks, dating to 1913. Thus, in early 2007, on the eve of the crisis, French households' financial and real estate wealth (net of debt) reached €9.5 billion, six years' worth of national income. French wealth fell slightly in 2008–9, but started climbing again in 2010, and now exceeds €10 trillion. If we put these figures in historical perspective, we can see that wealth hasn't been this robust in a century. Today, private net wealth is still equal to nearly six years' worth of national income, compared to less than four years' in the 1980s, and less than three years' in the 1950s. You would have to go back to the Belle Époque (1900–1910) to find French wealth holders so prosperous, with wealth-to-income ratios on the order of 6-to-7.*

It can be seen, incidentally, that wealth owners' current prosperity isn't simply due to deregulation. It's also, and chiefly, a long-term catch-up phenomenon after the violent shocks of the early twentieth century, as well as a phenomenon linked to the slow growth of recent decades, which automatically leads to extremely high wealth-to-income ratios. The enduring fact is that we live in an era when wealth in the rich countries does very well, while production and incomes grow slowly. During the postwar decades, we mistakenly believed we'd moved on to a new stage of capitalism, a sort of capitalism without capital. In reality, it was only a passing phase, reflecting an era of capitalist reconstruction.

---

* See Thomas Piketty, 'On the Long-Run Evolution of Inheritance: France 1820–2050,' *Quarterly Journal of Economics* 126, no. 3 (2011), available at Thomas Piketty staff page, Paris School of Economics, piketty. pse.ens.fr.

In the long run, patrimonial capitalism is the only kind that can exist.

Nevertheless, the deregulation that has taken place since the 1980s and '90s created an additional problem: it left the financial system, and the patrimonial capitalism of the early twenty-first century, particularly fragile, volatile, and unpredictable. Whole swaths of the financial sector grew with no oversight, no prudential regulation, and no accounting worthy of the name. Even the most basic international financial statistics are marred by systematic shortcomings. For example, at the world level, net financial positions are negative overall, which is logically impossible unless we assume that, when averaged out, we're owned by the planet Mars . . . More likely, as the economist Gabriel Zucman has shown,[*] this inconsistency suggests that a nonnegligible share of financial assets is held in tax havens by nonresidents and not correctly recorded as such. Among other things, that affects the net external position of the Eurozone, which is far more positive than the official statistics suggest. And for a simple reason: well-off Europeans have an interest in hiding their assets, and at the moment, the European Union isn't doing what it should – and can – to deter them.

More generally, Europe's political fragmentation and its inability to unite are particularly debilitating as it faces the instability and opacity of the financial system. When it comes to imposing the necessary prudential rules and tax laws on globalized markets and financial institutions, the

[*] See Gabriel Zucman, 'The Missing Wealth of Nations: Are Europe and the U.S. Net Debtors or Net Creditors?' Paris School of Economics, 2011, available at www.parisschoolofeconomics.eu/zucman-gabriel/.

nineteenth-century European nation-state is, obviously, no longer the right level at which to act.

Europe suffers from an additional problem. Its currency, the euro, and its central bank, the ECB, were designed in the late 1980s and early 1990s (euro banknotes went into circulation in January 2002, but the Maastricht Treaty, creating the European Union, was ratified in France in September 1992), at a time when many imagined the only role for central banks was to watch from the sidelines – that is, to ensure that inflation stays low and the money supply grows at roughly the same rate as the economy. After the stagflation of the 1970s, policymakers and public opinion became convinced that central banks had to be, above all, independent of governments, with the sole objective of targeting low inflation. That's how, for the first time in history, we managed to create a currency without a state and a central bank without a government.

Along the way, we forgot that during major economic and financial crises, central banks are an indispensable tool for stabilizing financial markets and avoiding cascading bankruptcies and generalized depression. The rehabilitation of the central banks' role is the great lesson of the financial crisis of recent years. If the world's two biggest central banks, the Federal Reserve and the ECB, hadn't printed considerable sums of money (several tens of percentage points of gross domestic product each, in 2008 and 2009) and lent it at low rates – 0–1 percent – to private banks, it's more than likely the slump would have taken on proportions comparable to that of the 1930s, with unemployment rates above 20 percent. Luckily, both the Fed and the ECB were able to avoid the worst, rather than repeating the 'liquidationist' mistakes of the 1930s, an era when banks had been allowed to fail one after the other.

Of course, central banks' infinite power to create money has to be kept within bounds. But in the face of a major crisis, forgoing this tool, and this critical lender-of-last-resort role, would be suicidal.

Unfortunately, the monetary pragmatism of 2008 and 2009 that helped us avoid the worst, and put out the fire for now, also led us to think too little about the structural reasons behind the disaster. Progress on financial supervision has been very timid since 2008, and we've chosen to ignore the inegalitarian origins of the crisis: all evidence points to rising inequality and the stagnation of working- and middle-class incomes – especially in the United States (where almost 60 percent of growth was absorbed by the richest 1 percent between 1977 and 2007) – as having contributed to the explosion of private debt.*

Most important, the rescue of private banks by central banks in 2008 and 2009 failed to prevent the crisis from entering a new phase in 2010 and 2011, a crisis of Eurozone public debt. The important point to note here is that this second part of the crisis, which now preoccupies us, is happening only in the Eurozone. The United States, the United Kingdom, and Japan are more indebted than we are in the Eurozone (with public debt levels of 100 percent, 80 percent, and 200 percent respectively, versus 80 percent for Eurozone members), yet they experienced no debt crisis. The reason is simple: the Federal Reserve, the Bank of England, and the Bank of Japan all lend to their respective governments at low rates – less than 2 percent – which calms markets and stabilizes interest

---

* See Facundo Alvaredo et al., 'The World Top Incomes Database,' Paris School of Economics, www.parisschoolofeconomics.eu/topincomes/.

rates. By comparison, the ECB has lent very little to Eurozone governments – hence the current crisis.

To explain the singular attitude of the ECB, it's customary to mention the primordial traumas of Germany, which is said to fear a return to the hyperinflation of the 1920s. To me, this line of thinking doesn't seem very convincing. Everyone is perfectly aware that the world isn't menaced by hyperinflation. What threatens us today, rather, is a long deflationary recession, with prices, wages, and production falling or stagnating. Indeed, the enormous money creation of 2008–9 caused no significant inflation. The Germans know this just as well as we do.

A potentially more satisfying explanation is the fact that, after several decades of denigrating the state, many find it more natural to aid private banks than to aid governments. Except that in the United States and United Kingdom, where this denigration reached its zenith, central banks proved more pragmatic and didn't hesitate to buy massive amounts of public debt.

In reality, the specific problem we face, and the main explanation for our troubles, is simply the fact that the Eurozone and the ECB were badly designed from the start; so it's difficult – though not impossible – to rewrite the rules in the midst of a crisis. The basic error was to imagine that we could have a currency without a state, a central bank without a government, and a common monetary policy without a common fiscal policy. A common currency without a common debt doesn't work. At best, it can work in good times, but in bad times it leads to an explosion.

By creating a single currency, we put an end to speculation on seventeen Eurozone exchange rates: it's no longer possible to bet on the drachma falling against the franc, or the franc against the mark. What wasn't foreseen was that speculation on exchange rates would be replaced by speculation on seventeen different interest rates for public debt. Yet, to a great extent, this second kind of speculation is even worse than the first. When your exchange rate is attacked, you can always choose to get out ahead of it and devalue your currency, which at least makes your country more competitive. With the single currency, Eurozone countries lost this possibility. In principle, they should have gained financial stability in exchange, but clearly that's not the case.

There's something else that's especially perverse about the interest-rate speculation confronting us today, which is that it makes it impossible to arrange an orderly rebalancing of our public finances. The sums at stake are considerable. With a public debt around 100 percent of GDP, paying an interest rate of 5 percent, rather than 2 percent, means an annual debt-service burden of 5 percent rather than 2 percent. That difference, 3 percent of GDP or €60 billion in France, represents our entire budget for higher education, research, justice, and employment! So if you don't know whether interest rates in a year or two will be 2 percent or 5 percent, it's simply impossible to start a calm public debate about what spending should be cut and which taxes should be raised.

That's especially regrettable because European welfare states obviously need to be reformed, modernized, and rationalized – not only to attain balanced budgets and sound finances, but above all to ensure better public services, more responsive to individual situations, with stronger guarantees of rights. The Left in France must take the initiative on these issues, whether it's the modernization of our tax system (which is both complex and unfair, and should be rebuilt based on the principles of 'equal tax on equal income,' with-holding at the source, and the broad base and low rates of our social security tax, the *contribution sociale généralisée,* or CSG★), reconstructing our pension system (currently fragmented into multiple regimes, making it both incomprehensible for citizens and impossible to reform equitably and via consensus†), or the autonomy of our universities (a third key issue, which, like tax and pension reform, shouldn't be abandoned to the Right).

What to do? To put an end to speculation on the seventeen Eurozone interest rates, the only lasting solution is to mutualize our debt, to create a common debt (i.e., 'eurobonds'). In addition, that's the only structural reform that can allow the ECB to fully play its role as lender of last resort. Of course, the ECB could buy more sovereign debt on the markets right now, and that emergency solution will probably play a crucial role. But as long as the ECB faces seventeen different sovereign debts, it will face an impossible problem: which debt to buy and at what rates? If the Fed had to choose every morning between the debts of Wyoming, California, and New York, it would have a lot of trouble carrying out an orderly monetary policy.

But to have a common debt, there has to be a strong and legitimate federal political authority. We can't create eurobonds and then let each national government decide how many it

★ See for example Camille Landais, Thomas Piketty, and Emmanuel Saez, *Pour une révolution fiscale: un impôt sur le revenu pour le XXIe siècle* (Paris: Seuil, 2011), www.revolution-fiscale.fr.
† See for example Antoine Bozio and Thomas Piketty, *Pour un nouveau système de retraite: des comptes individuels de cotisations financés par répartition* (Paris: Rue d'Ulm, 2008), available at piketty.pse.ens.fr.

wants to issue. And that federal authority can't be the European Council or the Eurogroup. We need to take a giant step forward toward political union and a United States of Europe; otherwise, sooner or later we'll be headed for a huge step backwards – that is, a rejection of the euro. The simplest solution would be to finally invest the European Parliament with genuine budgetary power. But the problem with the European Parliament is that it comprises all twenty-seven countries of the EU, not just those of the Eurozone. Another solution, discussed in my November 22, 2011, column, would be to create a kind of 'European Senate,' bringing together members of the finance and social affairs committees of the national parliaments of those countries wishing to mutualize their debts. This body would have the final say over decisions on issuing common European debt (which wouldn't prevent each country from issuing national debt if it wishes, but national debt would not be collectively guaranteed). The important point is that this group would make its decisions via simple majority, like all parliaments, and its debates would be public, transparent, and democratic.

That's what would make it different from the European Council, which tends toward inertia and the status quo because it relies on unanimity (or quasi unanimity), and usually amounts to a private confab. Most often no decision gets made, and when, by some miracle, a unanimous decision emerges, it's nearly impossible to know why it was made. That's the opposite of a democratic debate within a parliamentary forum. A new European treaty that stays purely within an intergovernmental logic (merely modifying the decision rule in the European Council from 100 percent to 85 percent) would be inadequate to the challenge at hand. And it obviously wouldn't permit the creation of eurobonds, which will require far more boldness in the field of political union – a boldness that the Germans seem far more prepared for than the French government. We should take them at their word on this issue and make specific proposals. That is our challenge in the months ahead.

January 2012

I

Why Save the Bankers?

2008–10

After more than a year of rising financial turmoil beginning in 2007, the crisis reached a climax on September 15, 2008, when Lehman Brothers filed for bankruptcy. This period witnessed a series of unprecedented government interventions aimed at restoring stability to the markets, including the Troubled Asset Relief Program (or TARP, a proposed $700 billion bailout) and billions of dollars in below-market loans and credit guarantees extended by the U.S. Treasury and Federal Reserve to a wide range of nonbank financial institutions that had never benefited from such assistance before. Many asked whether these moves marked the beginning of a new era of interventionist economic policy.

Why Save the Bankers?

September 30, 2008

Will the financial crisis lead to the return of the state on the economic and social scene? It's too early to say. But it's useful to dispel a few misunderstandings and to clarify the terms of debate. The bank rescues and regulatory reforms undertaken by the American government don't in themselves constitute a historic turning point. The speed and pragmatism with which the U.S. Treasury and Federal Reserve adjusted their thinking and launched temporary nationalizations of whole swaths of the financial system are certainly impressive. And though it will take some time before we'll know the final net cost to the taxpayer, it's possible that the scale of the interventions underway will surpass levels reached in the past. Sums between $700 billion and $1.4 trillion are now being discussed – between 5 and 10 percent of U.S. GDP – whereas the savings and loan debacle of the 1980s cost around 2.5 percent.

Still, to a certain extent these kinds of interventions in the financial sector represent a continuation of doctrines and policies already practiced in the past. Since the 1930s, American elites have been convinced that the 1929 crisis reached such great proportions and brought capitalism to the edge of the abyss because the Federal Reserve and the public authorities let the banks collapse by refusing to inject the liquidity needed to restore confidence and growth to the productive sector. For some Americans on the free market right, faith in Fed intervention goes hand in hand with a skepticism toward state intervention outside the financial sphere: to save capitalism, we need a good Fed, flexible and responsive – and certainly not a Rooseveltian welfare state, which would only make Americans go soft. If we forget this historical context, we might be surprised by the U.S. financial authorities' swift intervention.

Will things stop there? That depends on the American presidential election: a President Obama could seize this opportunity to strengthen the role of the state in other areas beyond finance, for example in health insurance and reducing inequality. But given the budgetary chasm left by the George W. Bush administration (military spending, bank rescues), the room for maneuver on health care might be limited – Americans' willingness to pay more taxes is not infinite. Moreover, the current debate in Congress on limiting finance sector pay illustrates the ambiguities of today's ideological context. One certainly senses mounting public exasperation with the explosion of supersalaries for executives and traders over the past thirty years. But the solution being envisaged, setting a salary cap of $400,000 (the salary of the U.S. president) in financial institutions bailed out by taxpayers, is a partial response that's easily evaded – higher salary payments just need to be transferred to other companies.

After the stock market crash of 1929, Franklin Roosevelt's response to the enrichment of the very economic and financial elites who had led the country into the crisis was far more brutal. The federal tax rate on the highest incomes was lifted from 25 to 63 percent in 1932, then to 79 percent in 1936, 91 percent in 1941, then lowered to 77 percent in 1964, and finally 30–35 percent over the course of the 1980s and 1990s by the Reagan and George H. W. Bush administrations. For almost fifty years, from the 1930s until 1980, not only did the top rate never fall below 70 percent, but it averaged more than 80 percent. In the current ideological context, where the right to collect bonuses and golden parachutes in the tens of millions without paying more than 50 percent in taxes has been elevated to the status of a human right, many will judge those policies primitive and confiscatory. But for more than half a century they were in effect in the world's largest democracy – clearly without preventing the American economy from functioning. They had the particular virtue of drastically reducing corporate executives' incentive to dip their hands into the till, beyond a certain threshold. With the globalization of finance, such policies could probably be enacted only with a complete reworking of accounting disclosure rules, and relentless efforts against tax havens. Unfortunately, it will probably take many more crises to get there.

Two weeks after the U.S. Congress passed TARP, the European Union announced its own framework for stabilizing the continent's banks. In an October 13 statement, President Nicolas Sarkozy unveiled the French government's response.

A Trillion Dollars

October 28, 2008

Forty billion euros to recapitalize French banks; €320 billion to guarantee their debts; €1.7 trillion at the European level. Do we hear a higher bid? In racing to see who can announce the most enormous bailout plan, the governments of the rich countries are taking big risks.

First, there's no guarantee that this publicity strategy will quell the crisis and avert a painful recession. Financial markets do like big numbers. But they also like to know exactly what the money will be used for, who will get how much, for how many years, and under what conditions. Yet on this score, murkiness prevails. In truth, governments are behaving like the worst of the corporations they're supposed to be regulating. Every accounting gimmick is making an appearance, with special mention going to the French president. Annual flows are confused with stocks, hard cash with mere bank guarantees, single operations are counted multiple times. And everything gets added up: the bigger, the better.

We find ourselves in a grotesque situation where the American and French authorities are rushing to hand out public money, with no real conditions, to banks that don't want it. The €10 billion lent last week★ to big French financial institutions was supposed to stimulate lending, but the commitment is merely verbal. Yet there is a whole legislative and regulatory arsenal that could force banks to lend some of their funds to small and medium-sized businesses, which would have been worth revisiting and improving in the current crisis.

Next, and most important, this strategy, based on misleading announcements of numbers in the hundreds of billions, risks disorienting the public in the long run. After explaining for months that the public coffers are empty, that even the smallest cuts involving a few hundred million euros are worth making, suddenly the government seems willing to take on unlimited debt to save the bankers!

The first source of confusion that needs to be clarified comes from the fact that annual flows of income and production are constantly being mixed up with stocks of wealth, though the latter are far larger than the former. For example, in France, annual national income (that is, GDP minus depreciation) is around €1.7 trillion (€30,000 per capita). By contrast, the stock of national wealth is €12.5 trillion (€200,000 per capita). If we move to the American or European level, these numbers should be multiplied roughly by six: €10 trillion in income, €70 trillion of wealth.

The second important point is that 80 percent of total

★ On October 20, 2008, French finance minister Christine Lagarde announced a deal to inject €10.5 billion into six large French banks via a new state agency. – *Trans.*

income and wealth belongs to households: by definition, firms own almost nothing, since they pay out most of what they produce to wage-earning and stock-owning households. That's what makes it possible to understand how the initial shock caused by the subprime crisis, which came to about a trillion dollars (the equivalent of ten million American households each having borrowed $100,000), though modest in size compared to total household wealth, could threaten the whole financial system with collapse. Thus, the biggest French bank, BNP Paribas, reports €1.69 trillion in assets against €1.65 trillion in liabilities, leaving €40 billion in equity. Lehman Brothers' balance sheet was not much different before its collapse, nor are those of other banks around the world. The central fact is that banks are fragile organizations that can be devastated by a $1 trillion writedown of their assets.

Given this reality, it's legitimate to intervene to avert a systemic crisis, but only on several conditions. First, there must be guarantees that the shareholders and managers of banks bailed out by taxpayers will pay a price for their mistakes, which hasn't always been the case in recent interventions. Second, aggressive financial regulation must be put in place to ensure that toxic assets can no longer be sold into the markets – with the same vigor that food regulators use when supervising the introduction of new products. This will never be possible as long as we leave more than $10 trillion in assets to be managed in tax havens in the most opaque fashion. Finally, we have to put an end to the obscene compensation packages of the financial sector, which helped stimulate excessive risk-taking. That will require more heavily progressive taxes on high incomes, the polar opposite of France's current tax-shield policy,* which aims to preemptively exempt the best off from any effort to foot the bill. With that kind of a strategy, we will probably have to prepare ourselves for even more severe crises to come — social and political ones.

---

* The *bouclier fiscal*, or tax shield, was a controversial policy advocated by French president Nicolas Sarkozy in the 2007 election campaign. Adopted later that year, the law limited a taxpayer's maximum liability to 50 percent of income. — *Trans.*

Barack Obama's historic victory in November 2008 arrived amid widespread fears that the nation was sliding into a new Great Depression. Drawing on the parallel, an iconic New Yorker cover image depicted the first black president as Franklin Roosevelt, cigarette holder in his teeth, waving to the crowds from his Inauguration Day touring car. Like Roosevelt, Obama offered a message of hope and a promise to break with the policies of his conservative predecessor. Many wondered whether another New Deal was at hand.

Obama and FDR: A Misleading Analogy

January 20, 2009

Will Obama be a new Roosevelt? It's a tempting analogy, but misleading for several reasons. Most obvious is the profound difference in timing. When Roosevelt was inaugurated as president in March 1933, the economic situation seemed completely desperate: production had fallen by more than 20 percent since 1929 and the unemployment rate had reached 25 percent, to say nothing of the alarming international situation. After the calamitous Hoover presidency, mired for three years in a 'liquidationist' strategy aimed at letting 'bad' banks fail one after the other, ensnared in antigovernment dogmatism (budget surpluses until 1931, no expansion of public spending), Americans wanted big change and awaited Roosevelt like the messiah. That desperate situation was what allowed a radically new policy to be put in place.

To punish the financial elites who had enriched themselves while bringing the country to the edge of the abyss, and to help finance a gigantic expansion of the federal government, FDR thus decided to raise tax rates on the biggest incomes and estates to 80–90 percent, a level maintained for almost half a century.

Obama, arriving in office just a few months after the onset of the current crisis, faces a totally different situation and much less favorable political timing. The recession is still far from reaching the apocalyptic depths of the 1930s – which limits Obama's maneuvering room to impose revolutionary measures. And if the recession worsens, he could be held responsible, which couldn't happen to Roosevelt. Indeed, less sure of his legitimacy than Roosevelt, Obama has cautiously put on hold his plans to raise taxes on high incomes, while choosing to let the Bush-era cuts gradually lapse: the tax rate on the highest incomes will be modestly lifted, from 35 to 39.6 percent by late 2010; the capital gains rate will rise from 15 to 20 percent.

His supporters are already criticizing the inadequacy of his public investment and stimulus plans, too oriented toward tax relief for the middle class, popular among Republicans, not ambitious enough in terms of public spending. A 'bipartisan depression' is beckoning, the economist Paul Krugman wrote a few days ago in the *New York Times*. In Obama's defense, though, we should remember another essential difference from the situation Roosevelt faced. In a certain sense, it was much easier to broaden the field of government intervention after the 1929 crisis, simply because at the time the

federal government was practically nonexistent. Before the
early 1930s, total federal spending had never exceeded 4 percent of GDP; Roosevelt raised that to 10 percent by 1934–35;
it peaked during World War II before stabilizing at 18–20
percent in the postwar period, which is where it remains
today.

The historic growth in the federal government reflected
major public investment and infrastructure projects launched
in the 1930s and, especially, the creation of public pension and
unemployment systems. The task facing Obama today is
more complicated. As in Europe, the modern state's great leap
forward has already happened; now is more the time for a
rationalization of the welfare state than for its development
and indefinite expansion. Obama will have to convince his
fellow citizens that resolving the crisis and preparing for the
future will require a new wave of public investment, especially in energy and the environment, as well as social
spending, particularly in the area of health insurance, the
poor relation of America's weak welfare state. Let's hope for
his sake, and for the world's, that he manages to do it without
our having to go through a depression on the scale of the
1930s.

As the economic crisis deepened in early 2009, trade union-led protests and mounting public concern over inequality and falling living standards prompted French president Nicolas Sarkozy to convene a 'social summit,' bringing together representatives of unions and employers to discuss the crisis and how to respond to it. Following the February summit, Sarkozy announced that he would request a report from Jean-Philippe Cotis, head of France's National Institute of Statistics and Economic Studies (Institut national de la statistique et des études économiques, or INSEE), on the distribution of national income, or 'value added,' between labor and capital. Although the report would not be submitted until May, Sarkozy's announcement quickly stirred debate about how national income was being distributed between wages and profits.

Profits, Wages, and Inequality

March 17, 2009

In a moment of brutal crisis, it's a shame to waste time on pointless quarrels. The debate about profits versus wages as a share of companies' income has sometimes taken surprising turns. Anyone pointing out that these shares have been stable is accused by some on the left of arguing that income inequality in France isn't growing, even though these are two totally different questions – and that's crucial to understand if we want to adopt the right distribution policy. Since inequality is the real issue in this debate, let's state it clearly: inequality has exploded in France over the last ten years.

A study by the French economist Camille Landais shows this indisputably. Between 1998 and 2005, purchasing power rose by several dozen percentage points among the richest in France (20 percent on average for the richest 1 percent and more than 40 percent for the richest 0.01 percent), even as the bottom 90 percent have seen growth of barely 4 percent. There is every indication that these trends continued and even accelerated between 2005 and 2008. This is a new and massive phenomenon, unknown in the preceding decades: the trend is of comparable size to that observed in the United States since the 1980s, which resulted in a transfer of something like 15 percent of national income to the richest 1 percent and income stagnation for the rest of the population. How can the first fact be reconciled with the second fact — that is, the stability of the aggregate profit and wage shares?

Anyone who logs on to the website of INSEE, France's national statistics agency, can see for herself. If you add up all wages (including employer taxes) paid out by French companies in 2007, you get a total wage bill of €623 billion, versus €299 billion in gross profits (what companies have left after paying workers and suppliers), so that 'value added' (defined as the sum of wages and gross profits) was split between a 67.6 percent wage share and a 32.4 percent profit share. In 1997 the figures, in today's euros, were €404 billion in wages and €195 billion in gross profits, thus a 67.4 percent wage share and a profit share of 32.6 percent. We've seen the same stability around 67–68 percent for wages and 32–33 percent for profits since 1987. Unless INSEE got its sums wrong, the fact appears clearly established.

Equally well known is the fact that the wage share fell

between 1982 and 1987 (which came after the increase of the 1970s). But it doesn't make sense to seek an explanation for the inequality explosion that began in the 1990s in a phenomenon of the 1980s, and it hardly helps us resolve today's problems.

So how could inequality rise so sharply since the 1990s, despite the stability of the wage-profit split? First, because the wage structure has shifted markedly in favor of very high wages. While the vast majority have seen most of their wage increases absorbed by inflation, very high salaries – especially those above €200,000 a year – have experienced considerable increases in purchasing power.

We're witnessing the same phenomenon as in the United States: executives take control and vote themselves exorbitant incomes unrelated to their productivity (which is unobservable by definition), encouraged by repeated tax cuts. What's more, in the financial sector these obscene salaries have incited senseless risk-taking behavior, which clearly contributed to the current crisis.

The only credible answer to this problem is higher taxes on very large incomes – a solution that's starting to emerge in the United States and the United Kingdom, and will surely reach France if Nicolas Sarkozy ever manages to see that the tax-shield policy was the greatest mistake of his term.

The second explanation is that the much-discussed stability of the wage-profit split doesn't take into account increased levies on labor (especially payroll taxes for social insurance) or the fall in taxes on capital (particularly the profit tax). If we look at the incomes actually pocketed by households, we find that the capital income share (dividends, interest, rent) has risen continually while the after-tax wage share has dropped relentlessly, making the growth of inequality that much

worse. Not to mention that companies doped up by the stock
market bubble and its illusory (and undertaxed) capital gains
have doubled their dividend payouts in the last twenty years,
to the point where their ability to self-finance their operations has gone negative (retained profits, which are less than
half of gross profits, are not even enough to replace worn-out
capital). The answer, again, lies in the tax system and requires
a rebalancing between labor and capital – for example, by
subjecting business profits to family-benefit and national
health contributions. This enormous job of construction will
require strong international coordination. Let's hope the crisis at least leads to a change in this direction.

Tax competition – the practice of attracting international business by undercutting other countries' tax rates – has long been an issue of debate in Europe, especially in relatively high-tax countries like France. The economic crisis revived the controversy over 'tax dumping,' as critics call it, especially after the 2008 economic collapse of one of its most conspicuous European practitioners: Ireland.

The Irish Disaster

April 14, 2009

Though it passed almost unnoticed in France, the new austerity plan introduced by the Irish government on April 7 tells us more about the crisis and its consequences than the recent G-20 summit. What's it all about? Like other small countries that went all in on real estate and finance, Ireland today is in a catastrophic situation. The bursting of the housing and stock market bubbles led to a collapse in construction and finance activity, and then in the whole Irish economy. GDP fell 3 percent in 2008, and the latest government forecasts point to an 8 percent decline in 2009 and 3 percent in 2010, before the beginnings of a recovery in 2011. Tax receipts have cratered, spending aimed at saving the banks and helping the unemployed (the unemployment rate will reach 15 percent by the end of this year) has increased, and as a result the country finds itself with a colossal deficit, forecast to be 13 percent of GDP in 2009 – equal to the entire cost of public sector wages and pensions.

The Irish government has been putting through austerity plans right and left. Already in February, public sector wages were cut by 7.5 percent to fund the pension system. This extremely brutal measure was justified by pointing to both the desperate budget situation and the coming deflation (the government forecasts that prices will fall by 4 percent in 2009, but workers haven't caught a glimpse of it yet). And last Tuesday the finance minister, Brian Lenihan, announced draconian new measures aimed at reducing the 2009 deficit from 13 to 11 percent of GDP, including an across-the-board income tax hike. The hit will be roughly 4 percent of total income, ranging from 2 percent for minimum-wage incomes (a €300 hit on annual incomes of €15,000) to 9 percent for the highest incomes, effective May 1. All signs are that this new austerity plan won't be the last.

What's most striking is that in an atmosphere of extreme crisis, the government is doing everything it can to keep its ultralow 12.5 percent tax rate on corporate profits. Lenihan said it again on April 7: It's out of the question to go back on the strategy that's made the country rich since the 1990s by attracting foreign investments and multinational corporate headquarters. Better to hit the Irish population deeply than to risk losing everything by causing foreign capital to flee. It's hard to predict how the Irish will react in the European elections: rejecting the government, rejecting the outside world, or even rejecting both at once. But one thing is certain: Ireland, by itself, will not get out of the awful spiral that the international financial system has put it in.

The development strategy based on tax dumping, which so many small countries have adopted, is a disaster. Many others followed Ireland down this path and can't turn back all by themselves. Almost every country in eastern Europe now has tax rates on corporate profits of barely 10 percent. In 2008 the computer giant Dell announced it was closing its local production units and reopening them in Poland, causing panic in Ireland. Besides, piling up foreign-capital investments comes with a high price: right now, a country like Ireland pays out roughly 20 percent of its domestic production to the foreign owners of its offices and factories, in the form of profits and dividends. In technical terms, the actual gross national product (GNP) of the Irish is about 20 percent smaller than their GDP. The cherry on the cake: the euro doesn't even let Ireland avoid paying exorbitant interest rates on its public debt. Ten-year interest rates in Ireland and Greece are now almost twice as high as in Germany (5.7 percent versus 3.1 percent), an utterly aberrant phenomenon for countries sharing the same currency, which shows that the markets are speculating on these countries' bankruptcy, or even an explosion of the monetary union. The International Monetary Fund is certainly equipped to put out this kind of fire temporarily by injecting emergency financial aid, as it already did in Hungary. But only the European Union can hope to have the political legitimacy to deal with the causes that led to these disasters. Basically, the deal would be as follows: the EU would guarantee financial stability in the zone and come to the aid of small countries if needed; but in exchange, they would give up their strategy of tax dumping, with, for example, minimum corporate tax rates on the order of 30–40 percent. After agreeing to give up their monetary sovereignty, the small and the large countries will thus have to agree to give up their tax sovereignty. Any other solution would be fragile. Building a monetary union without an economic government was risky even in the calm years. But faced with a major crisis, the risk of general collapse has to be taken more seriously.

The financial crisis set off a flurry of unusual emergency policy interventions by central banks. The numbers involved were large and the details often bewildering. In November 2008 the Federal Reserve launched its first 'quantitative easing' initiative, involving $300 billion in purchases of long-term Treasury bonds and a program of lending to financial institutions issuing mortgage-backed and other private securities. The European Central Bank was slower to move, but in April 2009 it opened foreign-currency credit lines with central banks around the world, and in May the ECB announced a plan to buy €60 billion in bonds issued by private banks. With central banks forced to involve themselves more deeply in private financial markets than ever before, concerns rose about whether the authorities would be able to stem the crisis.

Central Banks at Work

May 12, 2009

Not a day goes by without talk of the 'unconventional policies' that central banks are deploying to get us out of the crisis. Let's try to take a closer look. What do central banks do in calm times? They limit themselves to ensuring that the money supply grows at the same rate as economic activity, so as to guarantee low inflation – on the order of 1 or 2 percent per year. They also lend money to banks at very short maturities – often little more than a few days. These loans help guarantee the solvency of the entire financial system.

The enormous flows of deposits and withdrawals carried out by households and businesses never actually balance out perfectly, down to the day, for each individual bank. This lending role has traditionally been more important in Europe, given the importance of banks in financing the economy, which in the United States is more reliant on financial markets. What have the central banks been doing for the past year? Roughly speaking, they've doubled their size – a bit more in the United States, a bit less in Europe. Until September, the total assets of the Federal Reserve were about $900 billion, the equivalent of 6 percent of the United States' annual GDP. In late December they suddenly went up to nearly $2.3 trillion, or 16 percent of GDP. A similar trend can be seen in Europe. Between September and December 2008 the assets of the ECB went from €1.4 trillion to €2.1 trillion; that is, from 15 to 23 percent of the Eurozone's GDP. In the space of three months, central banks injected nearly 10 percent of GDP worth of fresh liquidity on both sides of the Atlantic.

To whom did the central banks lend this money? Mostly to the financial sector. But the main novelty lies in the duration of the loans granted to private banks. Instead of lending for a few days, the Fed and the ECB started to lend at three-month terms, even six months – hence the increase in the corresponding volumes. They also started to lend at these same terms to nonfinancial businesses, especially in the United States. Since the start of this year, according to the latest accounts published by the central banks, these lending volumes have begun to ebb. By May 1 the Fed's assets fell back to 15 percent of GDP, and those of the ECB to 20 percent. The central banks are betting that this means the financial sector no longer needs the exceptional liquidity, and that recovery is near.

But we could also interpret the reversal of these flows as a sign that the banks don't know what to do with the money. Indeed, financial-sector lending to households and firms hasn't really revived yet, and in the first quarter of 2009 it appears to have slowed at the same rate as it did the previous quarter. No doubt the central banks' unconventional policies at least prevented the cascading bank failures that marked the Great Depression, when central banks were inert. There's now talk of the possibility of innovative new monetary policies, with loans to the banking sector of up to nine or twelve months and direct purchases of relatively long-term bonds. The size taken on by central-bank balance sheets is still far from posing a real inflationary threat. Let's remember that the loans granted by the Bank of France at the end of World War II significantly exceeded 100 percent of that era's GDP, and 80 percent was lent directly to the government – hence the high inflation of the years that followed.

But unless we envision central banks starting to lend directly at all maturities and to every kind of economic actor, a task for which they are ill equipped, these unconventional policies will sooner or later reach their limits. Central banks don't have the power to force private actors traumatized by crisis to spend money. In practice, what last fall's monetary expansion mainly did was finance public deficits: the central banks didn't lend directly to governments (the ECB is expressly forbidden to do so by European treaties, and the Fed has reduced its holdings of Treasury bonds), but private banks have done so in their place. If it turns out that the state is the only actor capable of spending, governments will have to assume their responsibilities and launch a genuine stimulus.

One of the more notable events of the 2007 French presidential election campaign was the Pacte écologique, a pledge signed by all the leading candidates — including future president Nicolas Sarkozy — at the urging of some of France's best-known environmental activists. In June 2009 Sarkozy's government called for a national debate on the pact's most important plank, a tax on carbon, and appointed a conference of experts to study the matter. Over the following weeks, debate over the carbon tax reached a climax.

Mysteries of the Carbon Tax

July 7, 2009

Do you understand anything about the carbon tax? Congratulations: you're probably a seasoned environmental activist! Because for ordinary mortals, the plans now under discussion are surrounded by a number of mysteries that haven't yet been clarified in public debate. When it comes to the basic principles, everything seems clear. It's about taxing each form of energy consumption according to its volume of CO_2 emissions. With a 'double dividend' to boot: by taxing polluting forms of energy more, we could tax labor less, revolutionizing our tax system.

Things get more complicated when we look at the specific plans being discussed for 2010, which are hard to distinguish from a simple hike in the gas tax, something that has been done many times in the past. In fact, the new carbon-tax revenues being forecast for 2010 amount to about €9 billion,

€5 billion of which are to come from higher auto-fuel taxes, a sum that will just make up for the gas-tax revenue that was lost over the past few years. That revenue went from €25 billion in 2002–3 to less than €20 billion today, after gas prices rose and consumption fell. Making up for those lost revenues is a good idea, no doubt, but is it really revolutionary? The truth is that France has had green taxes for a long time: according to Eurostat, the EU statistics agency, ecotaxes bring in about 2.5 percent of GDP in total (half of which comes from the gas tax), versus roughly 3 percent in Sweden and Europe as a whole.

So what is genuinely new in the current plan?

In principle, what distinguishes a successful 'carbon tax' from traditional environmental taxes is that it's wholly guided by coherent ecological objectives, not by political or budget considerations. This has two crucial consequences. First, it's absolutely essential that all forms of energy be taxed at rates that depend on the amount of pollution they create. Until now, France has had relatively heavy taxes on gas, but has notoriously undertaxed natural gas, home heating oil, and coal.

Second, and more important, once this general framework is set and accepted by everyone, what makes a carbon tax different is that its level gradually rises over the following decades, based on an objective evaluation of the cost of pollution for society, a cost measured by the famous 'price of a ton of CO_2.' This hypothetical price is estimated by taking into account both the costs arising from emissions reductions (for example, if it costs €100 to plant the trees needed to absorb a ton of CO_2, or to develop a clean technology, then the price per ton is set at €100) and the costs arising from the emissions themselves (estimated on the basis of long-term climate forecasts and the consequences for human life). In France, the government's 2008 Quinet report on the 'reference value of carbon' proposed gradually moving the price of a ton of CO_2 from €32 in 2010 to €100 in 2030, then €200 in 2050. What that means in concrete terms is that the amount of carbon taxation will increase accordingly. Those figures are very uncertain and will obviously be revised and corrected. But the important point is that society and future governments would be committed to them increasing, whatever the short-term vagaries of budgets or politics.

A number of experts have also made the case that a creditable carbon tax must be an addition to, and not a substitute for, the ecotaxes already in place. In particular, they argue that the current level of the gas tax is only just sufficient to compensate for the other types of pollution linked to automobiles (air quality, congestion, noise pollution), but not for their greenhouse gas emissions. The technical argument holds up, but it has to be explained; otherwise the danger is that all this will look to taxpayers more like a double penalty than a double dividend.

This is especially the case because so far the debate over how to use the revenues from a carbon tax has gotten off to an extremely bad start. From the beginning, industrial companies were exempted from the new tax on the grounds that they're already part of the European emission quota system. Again, there are good technical arguments for this kind of dual tax and quota system. But it potentially undermines society's acceptance of the overall system, because at the moment those quotas are granted practically free of charge, and are only set to be auctioned off for a price starting in 2013. Under the circumstances, proposing to use carbon-tax revenues to eliminate those same companies' business taxes looks like an especially unwelcome ideological provocation.

In 2009 and 2010 the French press — tabloid and highbrow alike — were gripped by the family turmoil surrounding Liliane Bettencourt, the elderly billionaire businesswoman and heiress to the L'Oréal fortune. Not only was the story replete with human drama and courtroom fireworks, but, coming at a moment of economic crisis and mounting concern over social inequality in France, it also offered a revealing glimpse into the financial machinations of France's wealthy elite.

Lessons for the Tax System from the Bettencourt Affair

September 8, 2009

For a long time Liliane Bettencourt was merely the richest person in France. Now, with her daughter's trial, she represents more than that. In an admittedly extreme way, this affair perfectly illustrates some of the thorniest problems that the issues of wealth and inheritance will pose in the twenty-first century.

Let's review. Eighty-seven-year-old Liliane, heiress to the L'Oréal company, made a certain number of gifts to a sixty-one-year-old photographer friend, amounting to an estimated €1 billion, which comes to less than 10 percent of her total fortune (€15 billion). Her only daughter, fifty-eight-year-old Françoise, scolded Liliane for letting herself be taken advantage of, and filed a complaint for *'abus de faiblesse'* (exploitation of weakness). As for Liliane, she considers herself to be of perfectly sound mind, and resents her daughter's attempt to have the courts impose a medical examination. We should add that both women serve on the board of directors of L'Oréal, the jewel of the French stock market.

This is obviously not the place to opine on the mental health of the various protagonists. But there's no harm in pointing out that this story looks a lot like a civil war among the elderly – an old people's story, as it were. Indeed, wealth in France keeps getting older, an obvious consequence of longer life expectancy, but also of the fact that returns to capital over the last thirty years have sharply exceeded the growth rate of output and of the income accruing to those who work. Even worse, this trend is exacerbated by the growing pressure of taxes on labor incomes, which limits the savings potential of those who can rely on nothing but their work to accumulate something. Meanwhile, wealth holdings have benefited from repeated tax breaks, both at the point of bequest (gifts, inheritances) and at the level of capital income flows (dividends, interest, rents, capital gains). From this perspective, the sharp cut in the estate tax passed in 2007 – flagrantly contradicting all the presidential-campaign slogans about restoring the work ethic – represents a particularly harmful choice. Especially since by throwing away this stick, the government has, in most cases, weakened the carrots in the tax system that encourage advance bequests. In all likelihood, the main effect of the 2007 provisions will be to accelerate the aging of wealth that's already underway.

The Bettencourt affair also raises the issue of freedom of testament: the freedom to leave one's estate to whomever one wishes. Under the French Napoleonic Civil Code, inheritance is carefully regulated. Whatever their relationship with their parents, whatever the size of the fortune, children have a right to the *réserve héréditaire*. Parents may only freely dispose of what's called the *quotité disponible,* set at 50 percent of the estate when there's one child, 33 percent with two children, and 25 percent with three or more children. In other words, someone who has accumulated a €10 billion fortune (or who himself inherited it) has no choice but to reserve at least €5 billion for his only child, or €7.5 billion (split equally) for his three children. As it happens, Liliane Bettencourt followed this rule. But legally, even without bringing up her mother's mental health, her daughter could have prevented her from emulating Bill Gates, who has given most of his fortune to foundations.

Moreover, estates passed on within the *quotité disponible* framework are hit by much higher rates in France's estate tax: the goal is to encourage bequests to children – again, whatever the amount. Should we get rid of all that and move to an Anglo-Saxon-type system of total freedom of testament? It's a tempting option, especially since in practice that system leads to an equal division of property in the vast majority of cases, while still allowing the biggest estates to engage in philanthropy, whose dearth in France is often deplored.

Meanwhile, the Civil Code's protections for both disinherited children and exploited parents will be objectively strengthened by the increase in very long lifespans, so there's a danger that court cases like those of the Bettencourts will proliferate. At the very least, the *réserve héréditaire* mechanism deserves to be capped. Beyond a certain level of wealth, it's hard to see why the law should force parents to turn their children into rentiers.

In January 2008 President Nicolas Sarkozy announced that he had asked Nobel Prize-winning economist Joseph Stiglitz to lead an expert commission to investigate new statistical indicators of economic progress. Economic statistics had been a subject of controversy in recent years; some had argued that official data offered too rosy a view of the average French household's economic situation. The task of the Stiglitz Commission, the president said, would be to find ways to move beyond a narrow understanding of gross national product, which he termed 'an overly quantitative and accounting-oriented approach.' On September 14, 2009, the commission delivered its final report.

Enough of GDP, Let's Go Back to National Income

October 6, 2009

The Stiglitz report on new economic indicators has been criticized for lacking new ideas, and especially for offering recommendations that are as vague as they are numerous. It does, however, contain one concrete proposal that, though not novel, deserves to be supported. We should stop using GDP and emphasize NNP (net national product) instead.

Net national product, more commonly called 'national income,' was widely used in France before 1950, and still is today in the Anglo-Saxon countries. It can still be calculated from the detailed accounting tables produced by France's national statistics agency, INSEE. Unfortunately, it never gets highlighted, either in official publications or in public debate. That's a shame, and the reason can be summarized simply: in trying to measure the various incomes actually available to the residents of a country, national income seeks to place human beings at the center of economic activity, whereas GDP to a large extent reflects the productivist obsessions of the postwar decades.

GDP is a reflection of an era when the accumulation of industrial goods was thought to be an end in itself, and an increase in production seen as a solution to everything. Today it is high time we go back to national income.

What are the differences between GDP and national income? The first is that GDP is always 'gross,' in the sense that it adds together all goods and services, without deducting the depreciation of capital that made the production possible. In particular, GDP does not take into account the wearing out of housing and buildings, equipment and computers, and so on. Yet INSEE makes meticulous estimates of this depreciation, which are obviously imperfect but which at least have the virtue of existing. In 2008 the total was estimated at €270 billion, versus a GDP of €1.95 trillion, hence a net domestic product of €1.68 trillion.

Taking depreciation into account allows us to see, for instance, that French companies are currently in a situation of negative saving: they distribute more to their shareholders than they actually have to distribute, so that what they have left over is not even enough to replace used-up capital.

Many countries have also started to integrate depreciation of natural capital into their estimates, along with the damage to the environment caused in the production process. These efforts should be pursued.

The second difference is that GDP is 'domestic,' in the sense that it tries to measure the wealth produced within the domestic territory of the country in question without worrying about its final destination, and, in particular, not taking into account the flow of profits between countries. For example, a country whose firms and productive capital are entirely owned by foreign shareholders could well have a very high GDP, but a very low national income, once repatriated profits are deducted.

For France in 2008 this correction hardly makes a difference: according to INSEE and the Bank of France, French residents own roughly as much wealth in their foreign holdings as the rest of the world owns in France.

France's national income is thus practically the same as its net domestic product (€1.69 trillion). But things are quite different in many other countries, and not just poor ones, as the case of Ireland shows. Scaled up to France's population, Ireland's GDP is more than €31,000 per capita, but its national income is only €27,000. Of course, this is still greater than the average income actually pocketed by French citizens, since it includes the value of goods and services financed by taxes (education, health, etc.), which is legitimate. But it does get closer. National income can thus help narrow the gap between statistics and perception. But only as long as we also publish the distribution of national income, and not just averages. The latest update from the top-income data series that we have created with economist Emmanuel Saez thus shows that the share of national income going to the top 1 percent of Americans has risen from less than 9 percent in 1976 to nearly 24 percent in 2007, a transfer of

15 percent of national income. Between 1976 and 2007, 58 percent of U.S. growth was thus absorbed by 1 percent of the population (this figure reached 65 percent between 2002 and 2007).

The concept of national income lends itself well to this kind of social accounting of growth, and that is not the least of its virtues.

In February 2009 Nicolas Sarkozy announced his intention to eliminate the taxe professionnelle, *a business tax that finances local governments in France. The TP was introduced in 1975 under a right-wing government, and at the time François Mitterrand, then leader of the opposition Socialist Party, denounced it as 'idiotic' because it taxed productive investment in an era when capital could move easily across borders. Parliamentary debate over Sarkozy's proposal began in the autumn of 2009, but the plan quickly ran into opposition on both the right and the left.*

Down with Idiotic Taxes!

November 3, 2009

It's easy to denounce the idiocy of a tax. For a simple reason: all taxes are more or less idiotic, in the sense that they all tax people and activities that, in the abstract, it would be desirable not to tax. Things get complicated when, having proudly announced the elimination of an idiotic tax, political leaders go off in search of new revenues to finance the spending that we all, by and large, consider desirable: education, health, roads, pensions. The exercise can then prove perilous – all the more so since with taxes, it's always possible to come up with something more idiotic. The recent debates over the *taxe professionnelle* marvelously illustrate this cruel reality.

Let's review. The TP is currently applied to the value of capital (buildings, machines, equipment) used by businesses.

Until 1999 it was also applied to a firm's payroll, until the payroll portion was eliminated by former finance minister Dominique Strauss-Kahn, in the interest of rebalancing the French tax system, which according to countless reports leans too heavily on labor income. Let's recall that, generally speaking, all taxes apply either to the factors of production (labor or capital) or to consumption. When they apply to capital, they might fall either on the stock of capital (as the TP does) or on the income that flows from capital (profits, dividends, interest, rents), as does, for example, the profit tax, which has both advantages and disadvantages.

Let's also recall that no taxes are paid by businesses: ultimately, every euro of tax is always paid by households. In this fallen world, there is unfortunately nobody except physical, flesh-and-blood people who can pay taxes. The fact that businesses are technically required to remit some of them – in other words, to send a check to the tax authorities – says nothing about their final incidence. Inevitably, firms pass on everything they pay, to their workers (by reducing their wages), or to their shareholders (by reducing dividends or accumulating less capital in their name), or to consumers (by raising prices). The final distribution can't always be seen with the naked eye, but one way or another all taxes end up being passed on either to the factors of production or to consumption. For example, businesses submit payroll-tax payments, calculated on the basis of their wage bill. It's generally accepted that this tax is mainly paid by wages, which would be higher if the tax didn't exist.

Another example: every quarter, businesses write checks for the value-added tax, calculated on the basis of the total value of a firm's sales, minus the total value of its purchases from other firms. This difference, called 'value added,' is equal to what a firm has to pay labor (wages) and capital (profits). It is sometimes imagined that the VAT is entirely passed through to prices. That's not true: like all taxes, the VAT is paid in part by the factors of production and partly by consumers, in proportions that vary according to the degree of competition in the industry in question, as well as the bargaining power of the various actors, as shown recently in the case of hotels and restaurants.

But let's return to the TP. In the proposed reform, the TP would now be applied to value added (wages and profits), and no longer solely to capital. That would result in a tax cut on capital and a new hike for labor and consumption, reversing the reform of 1999. It would have been more justified to keep the current base of the tax, which also has the advantage for local governments of being easier to localize and less volatile than profits. But only as long as the valuations of firms' buildings and equipment are updated – which, as with other local taxes, has not happened since the 1970s. In the little game of tax demagogy, the weakest seldom come out winners.

Who Will Be the Winners of the Crisis?

December 1, 2009

What effect will the 2007–9 world financial crisis have on the distribution of wealth? Despite what you often hear, it's unlikely that the crisis will lead to a lasting decline in inequality. It's true that the fall in stock market and real estate values primarily affects wealth holders. But those who have nothing but their labor are also hit hard by the deterioration of the job market. That's how things go in all recessions. The immediate effect is, generally, both a reduction in inequality between the middle and top of the income ladder (a fall in profits and supermanager bonuses) and an increase in inequality between the middle and the bottom of the distribution (a rise in unemployment). If we look at the medium- and long-run effects, things are even more complex.

The Great Depression was, of course, followed by a period of historic declines in inequality in all developed countries. In the United States the share of income captured by the top 10 percent had hit 50 percent in 1928. It then fell to 45 percent in the 1930s, and then 35 percent in the 1950s and '60s. Not until 2007 was the record inequality of 1928 regained, and even slightly surpassed. But there's no reason for this scenario to mechanically repeat itself today. The historical data series on top incomes that we have created with the British economist Tony Atkinson, which now tracks the annual evolution of inequality in twenty-three countries throughout the twentieth century, shows unambiguously that financial crises, as such,

have no lasting effect on inequality: it all depends on the political response to them. For example, the Swedish financial crisis
of 1991–93 caused no change in the trend of growing income
and wealth concentration, which had been underway in Sweden since the 1980s. In the years following the Asian financial
crisis of 1997–98, we even see a sudden rise in the share of
national wealth and income captured by the top 10 percent,
both in Singapore and in Indonesia. While the available data
are still imperfect, the most likely explanation is that the
wealthiest managed to take advantage of the financial chaos,
buying up the good assets at the right time. The biggest fortunes contain a larger share of risky investments, which means
that they do better in booms and, in principle, fall more during
crises. Except that when you have €1 million in assets (and even
more so with €10 million or €100 million), you also have more
resources to pay financial advisers and intermediaries than if
you have €50,000 or €100,000. On average, this second effect
seems to have been the dominant one in the Swedish crisis, and
even more so in the Asian one. And it's entirely possible that the
same mechanism is at work right now. The truth is that we
don't know much, given how inadequate our statistical appar-
atus is for studying these complex phenomena of financial
redistribution in real time. This is especially regrettable since
such forms of redistribution are playing a central role today,
given the political response to the crisis. In 1929 governments
let bankruptcies multiply, which led to sharp declines in wealth.

Today, governments support banks and large firms, which
has allowed us to avoid a depression. But without holding
accountable the institutions thus supported, this outpouring
of public generosity in many cases brings about a reverse
redistribution of wealth. After 1929, governments held
accountable those who had gotten rich while leading the

world to the edge of the abyss: big tax hikes on profits and progressive taxes on very high incomes and wealth, all manner of new controls over capital (strict financial regulation, rent controls, nationalizations, etc.). It was these political responses that led to the historic reduction in inequality, not the financial crisis in and of itself. Today, the issues are different from a technical point of view (stock options, tax havens, etc.), but they remain fundamentally the same. Left to itself, capitalism, because it is profoundly unstable and inegalitarian, leads naturally to catastrophes. Unfortunately, it seems that new crises are necessary for governments to fully recognize that.

Amid a weak economy and numerous scandals, President Nicolas Sarkozy's popularity was reaching record lows in late 2009. The opposition Socialists, under the leadership of Lille mayor Martine Aubry, were feeling confident about their chances in the coming 2012 general elections. Yet the party was internally fractious and widely perceived as inaudible in national policy debates. It seemed an open question whether the Socialist Party would even try to formulate a coherent alternative to Sarkozy's agenda before the next election season. It was even less certain what such an alternative would look like.

With or Without a Platform?

December 29, 2009

Is it possible to win elections with no platform? Most assuredly. The history of elections is full of episodes that end with political parties attaining victory and power, not because their policies excited the masses, but thanks to the opposing party's mistakes and the rejection that results. The problem is that one day, someone inevitably ends up paying the price.

Take the example of the Socialists' 1997 victory. With the youth-employment and thirty-five-hour workweek proposals, you can certainly say that the Left had something resembling a program. But it's not casting aspersions on the leaders of the time to point out that those plans had been cobbled together in a few weeks in order to unite the parties of the Left as fast as possible, following the surprise of President Jacques Chirac's sudden dissolution of the National Assembly. That victory was mainly a rejection of the opponent.

And the price was paid starting in 2000. Once these two emblematic measures were in place, the Left coalition no longer knew quite what to do or propose to the country, simply because it couldn't agree on anything. Pensions, taxes, higher education, labor market: on none of these key issues did the parties in power have even the inkling of a program with any hint of specificity. The public ended up realizing this, which quite probably contributed to the defeats of 2002 and 2007. Not to mention that measures cobbled together on the fly are often political time bombs. It shouldn't be taboo to regard President Sarkozy's triumph with his 'Work more to earn more' slogan as a posthumous victory over the thirty-five-hour workweek, an excellent reform in the long run, but a poor fit for the era of large-scale wage stagnation that France and the rich countries have been mired in since the early 1980s.

Now let's cross the Atlantic. For many American observers, there's no doubt about it: if Barack Obama found himself caving in to the lobbyists and watering down his reform of the health care system, it's because his preelection promises were not sufficiently specific. He hadn't really been elected on a program, hence his current weakness. Looking on from Europe, where we're more sensitive to the international dimension of Obama's election, we tend to be more forgiving of the American president. Obama certainly should have avoided using Republican arguments in the primaries to criticize Hillary Clinton's health plan, which was more ambitious than his. That no doubt would have lent him more weight today as he faces Congress and the medical industry.

Still, who could claim that in the homestretch of the campaign Obama should have risked frightening voters by proposing a complete public health insurance program, thus jeopardizing his historic narrow victory? The 160 million Americans who have private health coverage were simply not ready for a public program, which in the United States can only be put in place gradually. Not to mention the fact that sometimes voters expect more of an overall vision and an ability to adapt to changing circumstances than a nice catalog of policies they don't understand at all . . .

Politics is not an exact science, any more than economics, and the border between honorable and dishonorable compromise is always difficult to pinpoint. What, then, of the 2012 French election? It's rather tempting for the French Left to bet everything on the gradual decay of the Sarkozy administration, which, having already been rejected by a good part of the center and Right, now seems to be racing to the Far Right. Except that ousting Sarkozy, however desirable, would not hold the same international significance as George W. Bush's dismissal, and can't be an end in itself. Not to mention the fact that, while it's entirely possible the Left will win in 2012 with no real program and with a candidate nominated at the last minute, based purely on rejection of the opponent, the opposite scenario unfortunately remains the most probable.

So, in anticipation of a platform, Happy New Year!

Record Bank Profits: A Matter of Politics

February 23, 2010

So France's BNP Paribas, the biggest bank in Europe, just announced an €8 billion profit for the year 2009, matching its 2007 record. Some are already crowing. After all, isn't it better to have profitable banks than bankrupt banks? Of course it is.

But it's worth trying to understand where those profits are coming from. The earnings of the ten biggest European banks came to roughly €50 billion in 2009. If we add the ten biggest American banks, we reach €100 billion. Where do such profits come from, when the whole Eurozone was in recession in 2009? The most obvious explanation is that during the crisis, central banks lent money to the banks at very low interest rates, money that the banks could then use to lend at higher rates to others: households, businesses, and especially governments.

Let's try a little calculation, rough and imperfect, but at least having the virtue of illustrating the sums in play. Between September and December 2008, the European Central Bank and the Federal Reserve created nearly €2 trillion of new money (almost 10 percent of U.S. and European GDP). This money was lent to the banks at rates on the order of 1 percent, at maturities ranging from three to six months. The loans were, roughly speaking, rolled over throughout the year 2009: in February 2010, balances at the Fed and the ECB were barely lower than the record highs they had hit in early 2009.

Let's assume that the €2 trillion lent to the banks earned them 5 percent on average, either because they went on to lend at 5 percent to other players or because the money allowed them to pay off debts that would have cost them 5 percent, which amounts to the same thing. The margin produced would then be €80 billion (4 percent of €2 trillion), which is the equivalent of 80 percent of the profits the banks earned in 2009. Even assuming a narrower interest-rate spread, that would explain a good part of the profits.

That doesn't mean the central banks did the wrong thing: the new liquidity undoubtedly helped us avoid a cascade of bankruptcies and prevented the recession from becoming a depression. That is, provided governments now manage to impose strict financial regulations that prevent such disasters from recurring, demand accountability (and taxes) from the banks, and, to boot, unload the debt that the governments borrowed from them.

If that doesn't happen, citizens might logically conclude that this whole episode is an economic absurdity: bank profits and bonuses rebound, job openings and wages remain weak, and now we have to tighten our belts to pay back the public debt, which was itself created to clean up after the financial follies of the bankers who, by the way, have gone back to speculating, this time against governments, with interest rates of nearly 6 percent imposed on Irish and Greek taxpayers. Greek taxpayers who, for their part, unwittingly paid out €300 million in fees to Goldman Sachs to prettify their own public accounts.

Demagogy? No. Just an observation: to reconcile citizens with the banks, something more than grand speeches will be needed. Obama understood this, announcing an ambitious bank-regulation proposal. But he is politically weakened. In

Europe, the fact that the ECB continues to rely on the ratings agencies in its purchases of government bonds (the announcement that triggered the Greek crisis), even though nothing in its legal statutes requires it to, no longer makes sense in the current context.

With this crisis, the ECB has convinced Europeans of its usefulness: everyone understands that letting the markets speculate on the franc, the German mark, and the Italian lira would not have helped anything. It can now assert its autonomy from the financial markets, supported by a genuine European economic government.

Across the Atlantic, the public authorities have no such modesty: over the past year, the Fed has printed $300 billion to buy Treasury bonds, without asking the markets' opinion. Europe, too, should accept that 4 or 5 percent inflation is the least bad way to rid itself of this debt. Otherwise, European citizens will once again have to foot the bill. There's no guarantee they'll let that happen.

11

No, the Greeks Aren't Lazy

2010–12

As the Greek debt crisis deepened and the prospect of an international bailout neared, some European media promoted a derogatory image of Greek society. The right-wing German tabloid Bild, *the continent's largest-circulation daily, was perhaps most aggressive in spreading stereotypes blaming lazy, corrupt, and free-spending Greeks for the crisis. But prominent politicians around Europe were known to indulge in similar rhetoric. In 2008 German chancellor Angela Merkel famously suggested that the experts could have averted the crisis had they simply followed the wisdom of the ordinary 'Swabian housewife,' namely, 'that we cannot live beyond our means.'*

No, the Greeks Aren't Lazy

March 23, 2010

Apparently, Greeks are lazy people who spend more than they produce. Worse, they elect corrupt governments that manipulate the public accounts to coddle them in their illusions. If your neighbor or sibling goes around spending more than he earns, would you do him any favors by lending him more money? Isn't it time he stop his free-spending ways and learn some hard truths about working and earning?

Obviously, this kind of metaphor, based on the morality of the household and family (sloth versus work, the prodigal child versus the good father), is a classic trope of reactionary rhetoric. The rich have been stigmatizing the poor this way since time immemorial. There's nothing new under the Greek sun. Except that today, faced with the complexities of twenty-first-century capitalism and its financial crises, such moralizing metaphors seem to be spreading beyond the usual circles. When you can't seem to understand the way the world is going, it's tempting to fall back on a few basic principles. Given the extreme rhetorical violence of the media's attacks, it's gotten to the point where the Greek prime minister declared on his visit to Berlin: 'Greeks no more have laziness in their blood than Germans have Nazism in theirs.' Words that harsh are seldom heard from heads of state in a political union; they should persuade anyone who hasn't yet taken an interest in the Greek crisis to do so now.

The problem with these household metaphors is that at the level of a country – and for individuals as well – capitalism is not just about merit. Far from it. For two reasons that can be summarized simply: the arbitrary nature of the initial inheritance, and the arbitrary nature of certain prices, especially the return on capital.

When it comes to the initial inheritance, Greece is one of those countries that have always been possessions of other countries. For decades, what the rest of the world owns in Greece (firms, real estate, financial assets) has exceeded what the Greeks own in the rest of the world. The result is that the national income available to Greeks for consumption and saving has always been less than their domestic production (after deducting the interest and dividends they pay out to the rest of the world). And that makes it rather unlikely that they'll consume more than they produce.

In the Greek case, the gap between domestic production and national income on the eve of the crisis was about 5 percent (twice the fiscal adjustment now being demanded of Greece). In countries that have gone all in on foreign investment (like Ireland), it can exceed 20 percent, and even more in certain countries of southern Europe. One might object that these interest and dividend flows are merely the result of past investments, so it's good and right for Greek debtors and their children to pay out part of their production to foreign creditors. Sure. Just as it's good and right for the children of tenants to pay rents indefinitely to the children of landlords.

We could look at the debate over worthiness in a totally different light. Talk about the arbitrariness of the return on capital: this crisis mainly results from the fact that Greek taxpayers suddenly found themselves paying interest rates of more than 6 percent on their public debt. Greece's domestic production is around €200 billion. The ten biggest banks in the world manage assets of more than €2 trillion each. A handful of market operators can decide in a few seconds to impose an interest rate of 6 percent rather than 3 percent on a particular bond – thus plunging a country into crisis.

A system like that will lead us straight off a cliff, so appealing to household morality is not what will save us. Ultimately, to resolve the crisis, the public authorities will need to take finance firmly in hand. In Europe, we have to create a path to fiscal federalism. That path does not run through the IMF, but rather through issuing European bonds. And at some point through a revolution in monetary doctrine. To save the banks, the monetary authorities lent to them with no questions asked, at interest rates of 0 or 1 percent. They were right to do so. But after that, it's unclear how to explain to taxpayers (Germans as well as Greeks) that they will have to tighten their belts for years to repay high interest rates on their public debt.

In the spring of 2010, the debt crisis in Greece began spreading to other peripheral countries, and on May 9, European finance ministers approved a €750 billion bailout. But many worried it would not be enough. Market fears of sovereign default were becoming self-fulfilling prophecies, causing selloffs of indebted countries' bonds. This pushed up interest rates, bringing those countries closer to the very defaults that markets had initially feared. Meanwhile, the European Central Bank remained hesitant to act as a real lender of last resort to the Eurozone's governments.

Europe Against the Markets

May 18, 2010

The countries of Europe are piling up austerity plans. We're witnessing a proliferation of drastic measures, like cuts in public sector wages, that haven't been seen since the Great Depression. We were taught at school that such measures always end in disaster. Since they only worsen recessions, we'll most likely find ourselves facing even higher deficits than before.

How did we get into such an absurd situation, and above all, what do we do? The number one priority is to create a European authority capable of fighting the markets on equal terms. If that means submitting national budget bills to the European institutions, starting with the European Parliament, well then, let's go ahead.

It makes no sense to keep letting the markets – which don't even know how to put prices on financial products they themselves created – speculate on the public bonds of twenty-seven member states. By creating the euro, we thought we'd reduced the markets' room for maneuver. And indeed, the situation would be even worse now if the markets were betting on interest rates for the franc, the mark, and the lira.

But now we have to move on to the next step: issuing a genuine European public debt. That way, the EU as a whole could take on the excess debt created by the 2008–10 crisis, which comes to somewhere between 20 and 30 percent of GDP, depending on the country. That would allow each member state to strengthen its finances in a sustainable way, so that we can move ahead on a stable footing.

Given how obvious this solution is, we're gradually moving toward it. European leaders finally seem ready to get over their legalism and to show more flexibility in interpreting the treaties, which in fact allow almost anything in the face of exceptional circumstances. But things are moving much too slowly. We were a little hasty to rejoice over the €750 billion plan announced May 9. In reality, that amounts to barely more than 5 percent of European GDP. Not to mention the fact that the commitments are extremely vague. The only funding that's relatively clear involves the €50 billion (less than 0.5 percent of European GDP) that the European Commission will be allowed to borrow directly in the EU's name. Then there are some vague promises involving possible bilateral loans between governments, perhaps complemented by the IMF, which we could very well do without. With time bombs like that, we're not going to put an end to speculation.

The question of financing will also have to be clarified. Suppose the EU were to assume national debts equal to 20 percent of GDP. Out of what funds will it repay those debts? With each country contributing to the European budget in proportion to its own GDP, surely the snake would be biting its own tail, solving nothing. Rather than raising national taxes, we would need to establish a European tax (a 10 percent rate on European corporate profits would amply suffice, for example), which would be a step forward in itself. The key point is that a European debt issue would allow borrowing at lower rates. Especially since the ECB, which has already started buying up national debts, will have no choice but to support the operation by buying European debt at low rates. That's exactly what the American Federal Reserve has been doing since early 2009: by buying hundreds of billions in Treasury bonds, it's lightened the burden on American taxpayers, helping to end the recession faster than in Europe. In the current circumstances, there's no solution other than monetizing part of the public debt.

And despite persistent beliefs to the contrary, 'printing money' doesn't translate into massive inflation: when you're on the edge of a depression, the main problem is avoiding a deflationary spiral. Between September and December 2008, the ECB and the Fed created nearly €2 trillion in new money (10 percent of European or American GDP) and lent it at 0 percent interest to private banks. That helped avoid cascading bankruptcies, without any additional inflation. To save governments, the same must be done today. We'll most likely end up getting to that solution, but it will take some time.

Rethinking Central Banks

June 15, 2010

Can central banks save us? No, not completely. But they hold part of the key to solving the current crisis. Let's start from the beginning. There have always been two ways for governments to get money: impose taxes or create currency. Generally speaking, it's infinitely preferable to impose taxes. The price for printing money is inflation, which creates distributive consequences that are hard to control (those with slower income growth pay dearly) and unsettles trade and production. Moreover, once it's underway, the inflationary process is hard to stop and brings no further benefit.

In the 1970s inflation reached 10–15 percent per year, and that didn't prevent economic stagnation and rising unemployment. That lasting episode of stagflation convinced policymakers and public opinion that central banks should be 'independent' of political authorities, in the sense that they ought to limit themselves to slowly and steadily increasing the money supply to aim for low inflation (1 or 2 percent). Nobody went so far as to propose privatizing central banks (the Bank of France was the property of private stockholders until 1936). In both Europe and the United States, central banks remain entirely in the ownership of states, which determine their statutes, appoint their leaders, and pocket any profits they make. In simple terms, governments have given central banks a mandate that amounts to a low inflation target. The era of massive loans to states and the private sector

alike was supposed to be definitively over. Never again were
central banks expected to intervene in the functioning of the
real economy.

The world financial crisis of 2008–10 exploded this notion –
born of 1970s stagflation – that central banks should be passive.
Between September and December 2008, following the bankruptcy of Lehman Brothers, the two biggest central banks in
the world doubled in size. The total assets of the Fed and the
ECB went from roughly 10 percent to 20 percent of American
and European GDP. In a few months, to avoid cascading
bankruptcies, nearly €2 trillion worth of new liquidity was
lent at 0 percent to private banks, at longer and longer maturities. Why didn't this massive money-printing operation lead
to higher inflation? Surely because the world economy was at
the edge of a deflationary depression. Central banks helped
prevent a complete shutdown of credit and a collapse in prices
and economic activity. They reminded the world of their irreplaceable role. In the end, no one paid a price for their
intervention: neither consumers nor taxpayers.

No one paid a price, except that in the meantime states
accumulated deficits that will now have to be paid back.
These deficits are not due to the loans made by governments
to private banks (which were of limited size compared to
those granted by the central banks), but rather to the fall in
tax receipts brought on by the recession. To lighten the burden, the Fed, and now the ECB, have begun buying up public
bonds, thus lending directly to governments.

But these developments, which have been less than fully
acknowledged, are happening much too slowly. Clearly, after
several decades of denigrating the state, it feels more natural
to us to print money to save banks than to save governments.
Yet the inflationary risk is just as low in both cases, and it can

be managed. The ECB could take onto its own balance sheet a good part of the 20 percent of GDP worth of public debt created by the recession, at low interest rates, while announcing that it will raise interest rates if inflation exceeds 5 percent. That won't excuse European governments from the need to get their finances under control and, above all, finally unite to issue a common European debt, to benefit from low interest rates together. But if they go all in on drastic austerity policies, there is a high risk that it will lead to disaster. Financial crises are part and parcel of capitalism. And when faced with major crises, central banks are irreplaceable. Of course, their infinite power to create money must be kept within bounds. But not to fully use this tool in today's context would be a suicidal and irrational strategy.

*The solidarity tax on wealth (*impôt de solidarité sur la fortune, *or ISF), levied on the net worth of France's richest households, was established during François Mitterrand's Socialist presidency. A symbol of the French Left's commitment to social equality, the wealth tax had long been an ideological flashpoint. One of the signature measures of Sarkozy's 2007 campaign, the tax-shield policy (*bouclier fiscal*), aimed at limiting taxes to 50 percent of a household's income, effectively lowering the tax burden for many wealthy households subject to the ISF.*

*Sarkozy's administration suddenly became entangled in the Liliane Bettencourt affair in June 2010, when secret tapes recorded by the butler of the elderly heiress were published on a French news website. Not only did the tapes suggest that Bettencourt was using foreign financial accounts to evade French taxes, but they also revealed intimate and possibly illegal dealings between Bettencourt's family and Budget Minister Éric Woerth – who doubled as treasurer for Sarkozy's political party, the Union for a Popular Movement (*Union pour un mouvement populaire, *or UMP), and whose wife happened to be employed as a financial adviser managing Bettencourt's fortune.*

Does Liliane Bettencourt Pay Taxes?

July 13, 2010

Beyond the obvious issue of the government's conflict of interest, the Bettencourt affair is a perfect illustration of several fundamental challenges confronting contemporary societies: the aging of wealth; the growing weight of inheritance, a long-term trend that profoundly undermines the meritocratic ideal; and beyond all of that, the iniquities of our tax system. 'Social distinctions may be based only on considerations of the common good,' says Article 1 of the Declaration of the Rights of Man. By all appearances, the fact that Liliane, who is in her eighties, and her daughter Françoise, who is in her fifties, control the capital of L'Oréal and sit on its board of directors contributes little to the common good of France's economy and society. These are not entrepreneurs; they are heiresses, rentiers, who mainly busy themselves by fighting each other over money. A rational tax system – a fair and effective system based on the common good – should by all logic tax them heavily, so that their shares might be gradually sold to less rich and more dynamic stockholders.

But what's going on is exactly the opposite. To be sure, Liliane proudly announced that she'd paid a total of '397 million euros' in taxes on her income and wealth over ten years. Without realizing it, she was revealing that her tax rate is well below that of L'Oréal's workers, and everyone else who has only their labor to live off of. According to the press, her fortune is estimated at €15 billion. So over ten years, she paid the equivalent of 2.5 percent of her wealth in taxes; that is, 0.25 percent per year. Let's say her fortune, which is managed by the minister's wife, earned her an average return of 4 percent per year – which isn't great. That would mean her average tax rate over the last ten years was barely more than 6 percent of her annual income (6 percent of 4 percent equals 0.24 percent). How is that possible, and how could it be that, under these circumstances, Liliane Bettencourt could benefit from the tax-shield policy? Quite simply, because the concept of income used by those provisions of the tax code has nothing to do with real economic income. Out of ideology, and probably incompetence as well, the tax shield instituted by the current administration functions in practice as a machine for subsidizing rentiers.

Suppose that Liliane were to declare €15 billion for the purposes of the wealth tax. In principle, she should pay almost 1.8 percent of her fortune annually; that is, €270 million in taxes. With a rate of return of 4 percent, her wealth should generate a real economic income of €600 million per year. But Liliane doesn't need that much money. To pay for her butler, her maid, and so on, all she probably needs to do is pay herself €10 million in annual dividends from the profits of the company that manages her fortune (the rest quietly accumulating in said company). In that case, the tax authorities consider her income to be €10 million (and not €600 million). With a 40 percent income tax (that is, €4 million), Liliane would thus pay a total of €274 million in taxes, which is obviously more than half of her €10 million taxable income. An injustice, cry the heavyweights of the UMP: Liliane works more than six months of the year just to pay the taxman! Sure, Liliane works hard. So she'll be entitled to the tax shield, a €269 million check that, roughly speaking, reimburses her wealth-tax payment.

That is how the Lilianes of this world, perfectly legally, can find themselves paying €5 million in taxes on €600 million in income, a tax rate of less than 1 percent. By definition, the bigger the rentier, the less he needs to help himself to a significant taxable income, and hence the bigger the rebate. It's a neat idea, actually. As things turned out, Mme. Bettencourt received a tax-shield refund check for just €30 million, probably because her declared taxable wealth wasn't more than €1 billion or €2 billion – the rest of her fortune benefiting from the tax loophole for 'professional' assets, or being declared by her daughter instead (who was herself no doubt a big beneficiary of the tax shield). Rest easy, they've thought of everything.

On November 3, 2010, the Federal Reserve announced a second round of quantitative easing, its unconventional bond-buying program. The first program, launched in 2008, had been halted earlier in 2010, but concerns over disappointing growth rates now led it to announce the second round, which was quickly dubbed QE2. The plan aimed at purchasing $600 billion in Treasury securities over the following year.

Should We Fear the Fed?

November 9, 2010

The new action plan announced last week by the Federal Reserve has prompted a good deal of delusional thinking and intellectual confusion. Primarily, of course, among ultraconservative Republicans, those eternal enemies of the federal government. Supporters of the Tea Party have gone so far as to demand the abolition of the Fed and a return to the gold standard. More surprising is that we're seeing only slightly more measured fears coming from some European observers who are usually better informed. For the most extreme among them, the resort to money printing is a threat to world equilibrium. In *Le Monde* last weekend, the business columnist Pierre-Antoine Delhommais went so far as to question the mental health of Fed chairman Ben Bernanke. Good Lord.

Let's take a closer look. It needs to be said clearly: the world today is in no way threatened by a return of inflation, which is now less than 1 percent in both the United States and Europe. The Treasury bond-buying program announced by the Fed comes to a total of $600 billion, less than 5 percent of American GDP. The idea that that kind of money creation could push us into hyperinflation makes no sense. At most, it would generate inflation of a few percentage points, which in reality would be an excellent thing. Today, there's a far greater risk of deflationary stagnation, worsened by fiscal-austerity policies. In such a context, it's perfectly legitimate for the Fed and the ECB to lend money to governments, whose public finances have been devastated by the financial crisis and the recession. What central banks are doing is reducing interest rates on public bonds, thus somewhat alleviating governments' budget constraints, which is always a good thing in times like these. This can also halt market speculation of the kind we've seen in the Greek crisis. Clearly public deficits have to be reduced. But to do so too quickly, without the help of central banks, would be pure folly. It would only worsen the recession, defeating the purpose.

What's odd is that two years ago everyone was defending the central banks when they were bailing out the private financial sector, even though that sector had caused the crisis. Clearly several decades of systematically denigrating the state has left its mark. And it's ended up making us forget that central banks are not there to twiddle their thumbs. In times of serious crises they play a crucial role as lender of last resort. That role may well grow even bigger in the years to come.

Fortunately this reality is starting to be accepted in Europe. The board of the ECB, which can hardly be suspected of a fondness for inflation, overwhelmingly approved the decision of its president, Jean-Claude Trichet, to go ahead with his government bond-buying policy. The dissenting vote cast by Axel Weber, president of the Bundesbank, was sharply criticized, even in Germany. So now is not the time to be criticizing the Fed: we'll need the ECB to do the same thing in the months and years to come.

But although central banks hold part of the solution to the current crisis, we shouldn't exaggerate their power. Clearly neither they nor anyone else can change the fact that we're living in an era of historic catching-up by poor countries vis-à-vis rich countries. That is, it's a time when Europe and the United States are growing at 1 or 2 percent per year while China, India, and Brazil are experiencing annual growth rates of 5 or 10 percent. That will probably continue until the latter catch up to the former, after which the whole world will likely grow at a relatively slow pace. It would be better to get used to this unavoidable reality than to make the whole world pay for it.

In late 2010, worsening conditions in Irish credit markets led Prime Minister Brian Cowen to request a European bailout for his country. Although the immediate problem in Ireland stemmed from its government's earlier decision to guarantee the debts of Irish banks, the specter of a new European bailout, after Greece's earlier that year, raised the larger issue of how to deal with the prospect of further such crises in the future.

At an October summit in the French town of Deauville, German chancellor Angela Merkel, hoping to spare German taxpayers and tighten market discipline on governments, prodded French president Nicolas Sarkozy to agree to a joint declaration stating that future bailouts could involve the imposition of debt write-downs, or 'haircuts,' on private bondholders. Although the market turmoil that followed the declaration later prompted European leaders to walk back this threat, many observers later blamed the announcement for deepening the crisis.

The Scandal of the Irish Bank Bailout

December 7, 2010

First, Ireland was a miracle. Then it was a disaster. Now it looks set to become a scandal. The European Union is unlikely to lend some €90 billion to save Ireland's banks and its budget without first demanding an increase in its corporate tax rate — which is now 12.5 percent but ought to be at least 25–30 percent. First of all because banks and other companies head-quartered in Ireland will be returning to profitability, thanks to the European bailout plan. The least that can be asked is that those profits contribute to Ireland's taxes in some meaningful way. But above all because development strategies based on tax dumping are doomed to fail, and harm not only neighboring countries but also those who practice it. It's long overdue for the European Union to take the initiative and bring tax dumping to an end in exchange for the financial stability that the EU brings to the Eurozone as a whole – provided, of course, that it actually does bring financial stability.

In all European countries, taxes represent at least 30–40 percent of GDP and make possible a high level of infrastructure, public services (schools, hospitals), and social protection (unemployment, pensions). If we tax corporate profits at only 12.5 percent, that's not going to work – unless we massively overtax labor, which is neither fair nor efficient and also contributes to high unemployment in Europe.

It needs to be said clearly: letting countries that grew rich thanks to intra-European trade siphon off their neighbors' tax base has absolutely nothing to do with free markets. It's called theft. And lending money to people who've stolen from us without asking anything in return so as to ensure it doesn't happen again – that's called stupidity.

What's worse is that dumping harms the small countries that practice it, too. Of course, individually, each country is caught in a vicious spiral: as in an arms race, the Irish have an interest in maintaining a low tax rate for corporations as long as the Poles, the Estonians, and others are doing the same. And that's why only the European Union can put an end to this ridiculous zero-sum game. There could be an entirely European corporate-tax system, or a dual system with a minimum rate of 25 percent in each country, complemented by a European surtax of 10 percent. That would let the EU take over the extra public debt the crisis has created, and give national budgets the ability to move forward on a stronger footing.

Such a reassertion of control is all the more urgent because dumping quite directly contributed to the Irish bubble and the current crisis. In particular, dumping has given rise to massive artificial accounting games that leave Ireland's bank balance sheets and national statistical accounts totally illegible. The national accounts are now seriously distorted by enormous transfer-pricing flows (a practice that aims to locate in Ireland the profits of affiliates based in other European countries), the exact proportions of which no one knows. The scale of this opaque accounting has grown even larger than Greece's manipulation of defense spending and public deficit data. In both cases, it's up to Europe to set things right.

But only if we use the right tool. The Merkel-Sarkozy plan to signal that some sovereign public debts would not be fully paid back (i.e., haircuts) was clearly not a good idea. First of all, because if we want to make the banks and financial-asset holders pay for their mistakes, which is highly desirable, then it would be much better to have a 'tax haircut' (debts paid back but financial profits taxed via a European corporate levy) than an 'uncontrolled haircut' in which banks are sent into bankruptcy – an uncertain process where no one knows who will end up paying the consequences. Primarily because the big countries' strategy will just re-create a whole set of disparate interest rates for twenty-seven different European sovereign debts, which will only restart speculation. That undermines the whole logic of the single currency and the rationale for small countries to participate in it. It's urgent that French and German leaders start over and finally put forward an ambitious European vision for exiting the current crisis.

Japan: Private Wealth, Public Debts

April 5, 2011

From a European point of view, there is a fact about Japan that never ceases to elicit surprise and incomprehension. How can Japan have a public debt greater than 200 percent of its GDP (two years of gross domestic product) and no one seems to worry about it? What reality, what political choices, are reflected in that colossal debt? All these figures expressed in percentages of GDP, or in trillions – with which we're inundated daily – do they mean anything, or should we turn the page as soon as we see them?

To try to make sense of these figures, it's best to refer to the national accounts, which in most countries now also include the stocks of assets (real estate and financial) and debts held by various groups (households, firms, government, rest of the world), rather than just flows of production and income.

These accounts are certainly not perfect. For example, at the world level, the net financial position is negative overall, which is logically impossible unless we assume that on average we're owned by the planet Mars. More likely, this contradiction suggests that a nonnegligible share of financial assets held in tax havens and by nonresidents is not correctly reported as such. Among other things, this affects the net external position of the Eurozone, which is probably much more positive than official statistics suggest, as the economist Gabriel Zucman has recently shown. Well-off Europeans have every interest in hiding assets, and the European Union for the moment isn't doing what it should – and could – to deter them.

But we shouldn't be discouraged by these imperfections. On the contrary: it's by exploring national accounts that we'll be able to help improve them. As is always the case in economics, we have to accept the idea that we're starting from a very low level of knowledge; that's exactly what makes the discipline relatively interesting and the progress potentially significant.

Refusing to count always works to the advantage of the richest – and that of inherited wealth (always quick to defend itself) rather than evolving wealth.

Let's return to the Japanese case. The first thing to note when we talk about public debts is that private wealth is always much greater than debt (private and public). In Japan, as in Europe and the United States, households own real estate and financial assets (net of debt) on the order of 500–600 percent of GDP. Typically in our rich societies, national income is around €30,000 per person and average wealth is on the order of €180,000; that is, six years of income.

The second thing to note is that while the Japanese government certainly has a gross debt in excess of 200 percent of GDP, it owns nonfinancial assets on the order of 100 percent of GDP (real estate, land), as well as financial assets also on the order of 100 percent of GDP (ownership stakes in public companies, savings banks, and quasi-public financial institutions). So assets and liabilities more or less balance.

Nevertheless, the net wealth position of the Japanese public sector has become slightly negative over the last few years, which is actually highly unusual: a government can't start selling off everything it owns. By way of comparison, the French and German public sectors hold a clearly positive position, even after the crisis. In France, public debt is close to 100 percent of GDP but public assets (nonfinancial and financial) are in the neighborhood of 150 percent of GDP.

This Japanese exception is particularly striking because Japan – public and private sectors taken together – has an extremely positive net position vis-à-vis the rest of the world. Over the last twenty years, the Japanese have accumulated net foreign assets equivalent to nearly a year's worth of income. This imbalance between private wealth and public debt was already glaring before the tsunami.* It can only be solved by increasing tax pressure on the Japanese private sector (now barely 30 percent of GDP). Recent disasters should, by all logic, accelerate this evolution, constantly held back since 1990, bringing Japan more in line with Europe, with all the difficulties that will entail.

---

* The major tsunami that struck northeastern Japan, causing an estimated $235 billion in damage, occurred on March 11, 2011. – *Trans.*

Greece: For a European Bank Tax

June 28, 2011

Germany is right to want the banks and other financial institutions that lent to Greece, sometimes at very high interest rates, to pay part of the costs of the current disaster. But simply put, this needs to be done in an orderly, fair, and controlled way, through a specific European-level tax on the banks – not by a partial default of the Greek state.

What's the difference? It makes all the difference. The problem with default is the blind and unpredictable nature of the consequences. We start by cutting the value of all Greek bonds by a certain amount, let's say 50 percent: those who lent €100 will be paid back €50 (a 50 percent haircut, in the usual parlance). But since the banks already passed the hot potato thousands of times, often with multiple insurance contracts linking them to other banks (including the infamous credit-default swaps, securities that basically let investors play the lottery on the probability of a Greek default), and since some actors can own Greek debt without even knowing it (for example, in recent years many ordinary savers had 'packages' of European debt foisted on them in the fine print of their life insurance contracts), no one knows who will end up footing the bill. There's no reason to think that the distribution of sacrifice will be fair: in financial matters, the biggest players are often the best informed, getting rid of toxic investments just in time. Above all, there's every reason to think that the chain of effects on bank balance sheets will result in panic in the European financial system, even cascading bankruptcies. Especially if the markets start anticipating that the same strategy of default and 'uncontrolled haircuts' will be applied to the debts of other countries in trouble.

The big financial institutions, seemingly so powerful, are in reality extremely fragile: by themselves they own almost nothing. Their balance sheets contain colossal assets and liabilities (€1 trillion for a typical bank, which is 500 percent of Greece's GDP), leaving an equity base that's often very small (let's say €10 billion). The Greek default could cause terrible turmoil.

So France and the ECB are right not to want a default. But the French solution, based on a purely voluntary contribution by the banks, doesn't hold water. Basically the idea is to make phone calls to our banker friends, asking them nicely if they could roll over their Greek lending and hold Greece's debt longer than they'd planned. The other side of the bargain is left unspecified. This is not the way to settle European problems. On the contrary, France should use Germany's strong and legitimate desire to 'make the banks pay' to negotiate a real bank tax or contribution that would make the financial sector pay the cost of the restructuring that's underway.

The great advantage of a tax haircut, compared to an uncontrolled haircut, is that the tax base and the tax rate can be calibrated so as to ensure that only the banks which can pay are affected, avoiding any panic. And such a tax could be the embryo – modest but real – of a future European-level tax: it's in times of crisis, and to serve some specific need, that taxes are established. Although it's not stated so explicitly, this is in fact the basic idea behind the ECB's proposal for creating a real European finance ministry (can there be a ministry of finance without a tax?).

What might this tax be, concretely? If the contribution were calculated as a percentage of the Greek assets held by the various financial institutions, then the tax would be exactly equivalent to default and would produce the same harmful effects. Some banks holding lots of Greek assets but little liquidity could end up in the red. On the other hand, to ensure that only the banks that can pay do so, it could be decided that the tax would only apply to profits. The bank tax would then be a European supplement to the corporate tax, and potentially the germ of a real European corporate tax. We could imagine an intermediate solution based partly on these two tax bases. Or one whose base relies on each bank's equity position, which would have many advantages for both financial and prudential regulation. But whatever happens, this is the European debate we should be having.

On October 5, 2011, Steve Jobs, the CEO of Apple, died at his home in Palo Alto, of pancreatic cancer.

Poor as Jobs

October 25, 2011

Everyone likes Steve Jobs. Even more than Bill Gates, he's become the symbol of earned wealth, of the good entrepreneur. For if Microsoft's founder prospered from his de facto quasi monopoly on operating systems (though he did, after all, have to invent Windows first), the creator of Apple has multiple innovations to his name (Mac, iPod, iPhone, iPad) that revolutionized both the design of information technology and its use. Of course, no one really knows how much such individual geniuses contribute, relative to the thousands of engineers whose names have been forgotten (not to mention researchers in basic computing and electronics who didn't patent their findings), without whom none of those innovations would have been possible. Nevertheless, all countries, all governments, both right and left, can only hope for such entrepreneurs.

In the symbolic realm, moreover, Jobs and Gates embody the figure of the deserving rich, a soothing idea in times like these. We've come close to concluding that their fortunes ($8 billion for Jobs, $50 billion for Gates, according to the *Forbes* magazine rankings) are exactly what they ought to be in an ideal world, and that all is decidedly for the best in the best of all possible worlds. Unfortunately, wealth is not just about merit, and before we succumb to this attitude of reverence, it's worth taking a closer look at things.

An initial clue: Jobs the innovator is six times poorer than Gates the Windows rentier – proof, perhaps, that competition policy still has some work to do.

Even more irritating: despite all those great inventions, sold by the tens of millions around the world, despite the explosion in Apple's stock price these past few years, Jobs still accumulated only $8 billion, one-third the fortune of France's own Liliane Bettencourt (€25 billion to her name), who, never having worked, has made do with inheriting her fortune. In the *Forbes* rankings (which do everything possible to understate inheritance, through both their methods and the rhetoric surrounding them), we find dozens of heirs who are richer than Jobs.

More troubling still: above a certain level, inherited wealth grows just as fast (and just as explosively) as the fortunes of entrepreneurs. Between 1990 and 2010 Bill Gates's fortune went from $4 billion to $50 billion and Liliane Bettencourt's from €2 billion to €25 billion. In both cases, that corresponds to an annual average growth rate of more than 13 percent (a real return on the order of 10 to 11 percent per year, after subtracting inflation). This extreme example reveals a more general phenomenon. For mere mortals, the real return on wealth doesn't go above 3 or 4 percent, even less for very small wealth holdings (the Livret A, the popular French savings account, currently returns 2.25 percent, less than 0.5 percent above inflation). But the biggest fortunes, which can afford to take more risks and pay for wealth managers, get higher average annual returns, on the order of 7 to 8 percent, and up to 10 percent for the largest fortunes — independently of any work their owners might do, or any particular talent or merit they might possess. Basically, the rich get richer, full stop.

The same situation prevails for sovereign wealth funds, or university endowments. Between 1980 and 2010 North American universities with endowments of less than $100 million got an average real return of 'only' 5.6 percent per year (net of inflation and all management costs, which already isn't bad), versus 6.5 percent for endowments of $100 to $500 million, 7.2 percent for those between $500 million and $1 billion, 8.3 percent above $1 billion, and nearly 10 percent for the three stars, Harvard, Princeton, and Yale (whose endowments went from a few billion in the 1980s to several tens of billions each in 2010, just like Bill and Liliane).

The mechanism is simple but its scale is disturbing: if we project these trends forward, we'll end up with major divergences in the distribution of wealth, and thus economic power. The right tool to regulate this potentially explosive dynamic would be a progressive wealth tax at the global level, with moderate rates on small fortunes, in order to favor emerging entrepreneurs, and much higher rates on big fortunes, which grow all by themselves. By all appearances, we're still far away from that.

Observers of the European Union, both supporters and critics, have long bemoaned the complexity and, frequently, the opacity of its governance. Besides the alphabet soup of agencies and commissions, decision making has been criticized for following the norms of international diplomacy – characterized by secrecy, private bargaining, and the playing down of differences – rather than parliamentary democracy.

The Lisbon Treaty, which entered into force in late 2009, was intended to make EU governance more transparent and democratic, notably by replacing unanimous decision making in the European Council with a system of 'qualified' majority voting for most policy areas, and also opening many ministerial council meetings to the public. But when the Eurozone crisis arrived, most decision making ended up taking place in private meetings between heads of state in the Council, or in the Eurogroup (an informal subcouncil of finance ministers for Eurozone countries only). The appointed European Commission and European Central Bank played important roles, while the elected European Parliament was only peripherally involved.

Rethinking the European Project – and Fast

November 22, 2011

Let's say it straight off: the disastrous Sarkozy-Merkel directorate is on the verge of blowing up the European project. For two years now, these two have been announcing last-chance summits and durable solutions every month, which are then immediately belied by events a few weeks later. On October 27, it got to the point where we were asking China and Brazil to lend us money to help put an end to the Eurozone crisis. In the annals of the Sarkozy presidency's economic incompetence and political impotence, this pathetic appeal for help will surely remain unsurpassed, for the simple reason that it makes no sense for the richest economic zone in the world to ask for help from countries that are poorer than us.

The EU's GDP exceeds €12 trillion (€9 billion for the Eurozone), versus €4 trillion for China and €1.5 billion for Brazil. Most important, the total wealth of EU households is more than €50 trillion (including more than €25 trillion in financial assets); that's twenty times more than China's foreign reserves (€2.5 trillion), five times more than Europe's entire sovereign debt (€10 trillion). We absolutely have the means to solve our debt problems on our own – if only Europe would stop behaving like a political dwarf and a tax-revenue sieve.

It gets worse. Europe today is less indebted than the United States, the United Kingdom, and Japan, and yet we're the ones with a sovereign debt crisis. France thus finds itself paying an interest rate of almost 4 percent – maybe 5 percent, 6 percent, or more in the months to come – while those three countries borrow at just 2 percent. Why? Because we're the only ones whose central bank lacks the support of a political authority and an economic government, so that it's unable to fully play its role as lender of last resort and calm the markets. With a debt smaller than Britain's, we're going to end up with debt-service payments that are far greater. Europe should be there to protect us, not to make us more vulnerable and our budget problems worse!

So what to do? It is urgent to establish a new treaty allowing those countries that wish (starting with France and
Germany) to place their debts in common, and in exchange to
submit their budget decisions to a strong and legitimate federal political authority. What should this authority be? That's
the heart of the question that we urgently need to debate.

What's certain is that we have to move beyond the logic of
intergovernmentalism and little private confabs among heads
of state. Contrary to what we were asked to believe during
the debate over the now-defunct European constitution, the
Council of Heads of State will never be Europe's upper chamber. Nor would it make any more sense to delegate budget
authority to the judges of the European Court of Justice. Giving power to the current European Parliament is a tempting
solution (it's the only really democratic European institution),
except that, on the one hand, its 750 deputies have so far never
held any real financial responsibility, and on the other hand,
they come from the twenty-seven member states of the EU,
not just from the Eurozone.

One solution that's mentioned more and more frequently is
to create a new parliamentary chamber bringing together
deputies from the finance and social affairs committees of the
various national parliaments. This 'European Senate' would
have the final say over any European debt agency, and each
year it would determine the amount of borrowing to be
authorized. It would have the advantage of being both smaller
than the European Parliament and of bringing together people who will have to assume the political consequences of
their decisions within each country.

That may be the right solution. If it is, a precise plan
needs to be put on the table quickly, with the chamber's size
and composition, the procedures for voting and appointing

members, and so on, all detailed. Whatever happens, it's crucial to find a solution that will allow the body to start
functioning very fast, with however many countries so wish,
while looking toward the gradual entry of all those who
would like to join this core federal group to benefit from a
mutualized European debt.

And we have to stop thinking it's the Germans who are
blocking everything. In reality, Germany – which is coming to
realize that it, too, is too small to regulate globalized capitalism –
is further ahead than France in its thinking about the necessary
federal leap. On November 9, Germany's so-called Wise Men
(members of the government's economic advisory council,
hardly known for its revolutionary tendencies) proposed that
all national debt above 60 percent of GDP be mutualized at the
European level, including, of course, Germany's debt. And it
was Merkel's CDU party that, on November 14, adopted the
principle of electing a president of the European Commission
by universal suffrage (an obvious finger in the eye to Nicolas
Sarkozy). In the current talks, every indication is that it's
Sarkozy who remains crouched in a purely intergovernmental
logic, refusing to cede an ounce of his power. It remains to be
hoped that, faced with the gravity of the situation, he finally
resolves to make the right decisions.

At the November 2011 G-20 summit, held in Cannes, France, President Nicolas Sarkozy pushed for a strong statement promising international action against tax havens, a long-standing policy priority for France. But while the resulting G-20 statement went further than previous summit communiqués in pledging to 'protect our public finances and the global financial system from the risks posed by tax havens,' it stopped short of specifying stronger countermeasures against such jurisdictions.

Protectionism: A Useful Weapon . . . for Lack of Anything Better

December 20, 2011

Why do the vast majority of economists believe in free trade? Because they learned in school that it's more efficient, in the first instance, to try to produce as much wealth as possible by relying on free and competitive markets to maximize everyone's comparative advantage. Even if that means, in the second instance, equitably redistributing the gains, through transparent taxes and transfers within each country. That's what economists learn at school: efficient redistribution is tax redistribution; markets and prices must be left to do their work, by having as few distortions as possible (this is the

famous 'free and undistorted competition'),* even if that
means redistribution later, 'in the second instance.'

Not everything in this lovely story is wrong; far from it.
Nevertheless, it raises a major problem. Over the past thirty
years, trade in goods and services has been profoundly liber-
alized, mostly in the name of this logic. But the 'second
instance' – greater redistribution – never came. Just the opposite:
international tax competition has hammered the progressive
levies that were patiently built up over the preceding decades.
The richest benefited from sharp cuts in taxes, even though
they were already the main beneficiaries of trade liberalization
and globalization. Those of modest means had to be content
with higher payroll taxes and consumption taxes, all in a context
of wage and employment stagnation. Instead of a more equitable
sharing of the gains from liberalization, tax redistribution has,
on the contrary, tended to worsen its inegalitarian effects.

Some will say: That's too bad, but what can you do? If voters' political preferences led them to choose less tax
redistribution, that might be regrettable, of course, but surely
we shouldn't reinstitute trade barriers, since that will only
slow an already lagging rate of growth.

Sure. Except, on closer inspection, unconditional trade liberalization and tax dumping work hand in glove. The public
authorities have been disarmed without getting anything in
return. In fact, by prohibiting import taxes and export subsidies, we've encouraged states to develop other tools to
promote their domestic production, especially through tax
exemptions for foreign investors and highly skilled labor (all
of this being entirely permitted, of course). Not to mention

---

* A reference to the Maastricht Treaty, the accord that created the European Union and paved the way for the euro. – *Trans.*

the fact that deregulation of financial services and capital flows has directly facilitated tax evasion by both businesses and individuals. Lacking sufficient coordination between countries, the capacity of states to carry out an independent tax policy has been sharply reduced.

One example among others: the EU Savings Directive introduced in 2005 was finally supposed to facilitate the automatic exchange of information between European tax agencies, so that each country would know in real time about its residents' foreign-asset holdings and the corresponding interest payments. Except that it still doesn't apply to Luxembourg or Switzerland. Moreover, the latter country just negotiated a continuation of the exemption regime that allows it – perfectly legally – not to reveal the identities of its banks' account holders. And except that the directive itself only applies to bank accounts and bonds, thus excluding the bulk of large foreign financial holdings (notably stock accounts).

In order for this to really change, we will need something more than peaceful G-20 summits and declarations of good intentions. To force the tax havens' hands and, more generally, to institute the financial, social, and environmental regulations we need to take control of a globalized capitalism gone mad, trade will surely be an indispensable weapon. If Europe speaks with a single voice and stops behaving like a political dwarf, we can even avoid carrying out the threats of embargoes and protectionism. Which would be preferable, since while protectionism – like the police – is an essential tool of deterrence that states must keep at hand, it is not in itself a source of prosperity (contrary to what certain enthusiastic 'de-globalizers' might think). But if we choose to deepen European integration without real advances in this direction, we run the risk of eliciting extremely violent nationalist reactions.

The 2012 presidential election in France took place against a background of economic turmoil, popular anger at the power of finance, and widespread discontent with the leadership of Nicolas Sarkozy, who had aligned himself closely with the austerity-oriented policy priorities of German chancellor Angela Merkel. The Socialist Party challenger, François Hollande, launched his campaign by declaring that his 'real adversary' in the campaign was the 'world of finance,' and promised to 'renegotiate' Merkel and Sarkozy's antideficit fiscal treaty, then awaiting ratification by the French National Assembly. Shortly afterward, he promised to raise the top income tax rate to 75 percent. Two weeks after his victory, President Hollande made his European debut at an informal EU summit in Denmark. The meeting was widely seen as a test of his promises to reassert France's influence in Europe and reorient the continent's response to the economic crisis. Although no decisions were made at the meeting, Hollande's advocacy of 'eurobonds' prompted a lively debate among the European heads of state, according to news accounts. Two days later, conservative Bundesbank president Jens Weidmann weighed in, in an interview with Le Monde. *He dismissed the calls for eurobonds, arguing that 'the main problem of Europe's countries remains the indebtedness of its governments, so we shouldn't be launching into a new round of public spending.'*

Federalism: The Only Solution

June 5, 2012

What will emerge from the European negotiations now underway? The danger is that France will take the easy route of playing the good guy, hanging responsibility on Germany if eurobonds fail. Even though, in reality, no specific French plan is on the table.

It might seem like things are clear: France is proposing to mutualize European nations' public debts so they can benefit in unison from low and predictable interest rates and be sheltered from speculation. Indeed, that's the only way to durably resolve the Eurozone's problems. As soon as each country gives up the ability to devalue its currency, it's essential to obtain financial stability at the federal level in exchange. Without that, the system will blow up sooner or later.

The hitch is that France is balking at the political consequences of such a plan. If we decide to create a common debt, then we can't let each country decide on its own how much of this common debt it wants to issue. The mutualization of debts logically implies a leap forward to political union and European federalism.

And the reality is that the Germans are ahead of us on this question, as can be seen by the CDU's proposal that the European Union president be elected by universal suffrage. In a recent interview, the Bundesbank's president found it easy to mock the supposed French stance on eurobonds, since the questions of European federalism and delegating sovereignty weren't even mentioned in the French election campaign, and French leaders are still ignoring the issue.

It's urgent, however, and solutions do exist. For Europe finally to become democratic, decisions on common debt must be made in a federal parliamentary forum following an open public debate. Private confabs between heads of state can't keep taking the place of European governance. But the European Parliament would be hard-pressed to play this role, both because it includes countries not in the Eurozone and because national parliament members can't have their budgetary powers taken away.

A concrete solution could be the creation of a new budget chamber specific to the Eurozone, uniting the finance and social affairs committees of the German Bundestag and the French National Assembly, and the various other countries wishing to move forward. The Eurozone finance minister, heading a European treasury, would be responsible to this chamber, forming a European federal government in embryo.

Contrary to popular belief, such an innovation isn't out of reach. Countries wishing to do so could absolutely adopt a treaty establishing these rules, while leaving others the ability to join later. Just a few months ago, European countries agreed on a treaty that settled none of the Eurozone's problems. With a few extra months, why couldn't they arrive at another treaty that finally would?

By letting the European Council president prepare the June 28 summit, the French government intended to put the supranational institutions at the center of the action, which is certainly laudable. But if France doesn't indicate exactly how far it's willing to go on eurobonds and political union, then the risk of failure is clear.

Especially since less ambitious, but comparatively specific plans have already been put on the table. The most detailed is the 'redemption fund' proposed in November by Germany's economic advisory panel. The idea is to mutualize all national debts above 60 percent of GDP (in terms of volume, Italy would be the most affected, followed by Germany, then France and Spain). The redemption fund would be financed by designated tax receipts from each country, contributed in proportion to the debts placed in common. When debts mature, the fund could borrow with a guarantee from all members, so that countries wouldn't have to face the markets alone. Initially rejected by Merkel, this plan has just been taken up by the Social Democratic Party and the German Greens, and is gaining more and more adherents in the CDU.

Envisioned as purely temporary, the mechanism has its limits. The 60 percent threshold and the size of the rollover create the risk that a country like Italy would be forced to return to the markets in a few years. The plan has no provisions for political union, which is problematic, given the consequences that the fund's decisions will have for national budgets.

But the proposal at least has the virtue of existing. France would do well to put its own plan on the table. By constantly putting off decisions on eurobonds and a federal leap forward, Europe is playing with fire.

June 29 saw François Hollande's first Eurozone summit, held in Brussels. Despite having initiated a debate over eurobonds at the previous month's informal EU summit, he did not raise the issue at the Brussels meeting.

The What and Why of Federalism

July 4, 2012

By putting off important decisions, the European officials who gathered in Brussels last Friday merely gained a little time. The prospect of a banking union, an important step forward, unfortunately remains vague. The question of eurobonds wasn't even mentioned. And the reason is simple: France had formulated no specific proposals on fiscal and political union that would make eurobonds possible in concrete terms. Three years after the start of the euro crisis, we continue to make believe that we'll solve it with more patch-up jobs and last-ditch summits ending with ritual late-night press conferences and cries of victory.

But the problem remains unsolved: What original and pragmatic form could European federalism take? Everyone can see that the euro won't survive in its current form. Yet at the same time, the federal leap frightens people, partly for good reasons that should be urgently debated so that these fears can be overcome.

In these pages (*Libération*, June 18, 2012), the economist

Bruno Amable recently argued that the federal leap risked being a 'deadly jump' for social protection. His argument, specific and frightening, is as follows. Europe's systems of social protection are fragile. They're the product of solidarity and specific national compromises that were patiently built up within the framework of nation-states. All of this would risk being undermined in the framework of a vast federal state, where ethnic or national conflicts often overwhelm class conflict. In concrete terms, the United States didn't develop a welfare state because it didn't want to subsidize a black underclass, and a United States of Europe would be in danger of dismantling its own welfare state because it didn't want to pay for the Greeks.

The problem with this argument, I think, is that in the context of European federalism we're under no obligation to make everything uniform and place everything in common. The rule should be simple: we need to place in common that which we can't do alone. Nothing more, nothing less. It would be entirely useless, and counterproductive, to fuse different countries' retirement systems. Even at the French level, we have plenty of trouble modifying the rules, unifying the different systems, reconciling the right to retirement with the right to lifelong learning. It's unlikely that the problem would get any simpler, or the debate any calmer, by moving it up to a higher level. The same is true of fusing the social security tax and the income tax, or instituting a four-day school week: for the most part, these debates and areas of jurisdiction should stay at the national level.

On the other hand, there are domains like financial regulation and tax havens where each country can't do much on its own, where the right level of intervention is clearly European. At the scale of the global economy, France and Germany are hardly bigger than Greece or Ireland. By remaining divided, we're putting ourselves in the hands of the speculators and tax evaders. This is not the best way to defend the European social model.

That's why it is urgently necessary to put Eurozone public debts in common, so that markets will stop imposing erratic and destabilizing interest rates on this or that country, along with the corporate tax, which multinational companies are evading on a massive scale. It's those two tools, and those two tools alone, that must be mutualized and placed under the control of the federal political authority.

In concrete terms, a new Eurozone fiscal chamber, made up of deputies from the national parliaments' finance and social affairs committees, would decide by majority vote on the amount of public debt that the European treasury could issue annually, after a public and democratic debate and on the basis of proposals from a European finance minister responsible to that chamber. But each national parliament would remain entirely free with regard to its overall level of taxes and spending, and of course, with how they're distributed. Concretely, if we decide on a European deficit of 3 percent of GDP, that in no way prevents one country from having 50 percent of GDP in spending and 47 percent in taxes, while another has 40 percent and 37 percent. Such a system requires a new treaty among countries wishing to move forward, but in no way is that beyond the realm of the possible, if only the political will exists – especially at the French level. Let's hope the debate on European federalism finally takes place in the months to come.

III

Can Growth Save Us?

2012–15

Merkhollande and the Eurozone: Shortsighted Selfishness

December 18, 2012

Why aren't France and Germany pushing for political and fiscal union in the Eurozone? For a simple reason: both countries currently benefit from extremely low interest rates (less than 1 percent) and are washing their hands of Italy and Spain, which pay rates above 5 percent and are sinking deeper into crisis. It's a shortsighted selfishness: we'll all suffer from the Eurozone recession that's setting in. Not to mention the fact that no one can predict the violent political reactions all this could end up eliciting in southern Europe or elsewhere.

At best, Europe will have wasted a decade bickering and not investing in the future. And this despite the fact that we have the best social model in the world, and ought to have the best universities on the planet, to win the battle for knowledge and sustainable development in the twenty-first century.

As for the little game of national selfishness, it's hard to know who's the most guilty. Germany racks up trade surpluses that are much too big: no one needs such reserves, and by definition such a strategy can't work if everyone follows it. But France, besides the fact that it's shown itself incapable of reforming and modernizing its economic, tax, and social systems, has actually made no specific proposals for the mutualization of public debts.

The only concrete proposal to date remains the redemption-fund plan, formulated just a year ago by the council of German economists who advise the chancellor. The idea is to place all national debts exceeding 60 percent of GDP in common. The plan is far from perfect. It entirely lacks a political arm: once the fund is set up, the annual deficit and the pace of de-leveraging and common debt issuance should be determined by a fiscal parliament of the Eurozone, after public and democratic deliberation − the opposite of the heads-of-state summits that have so far taken the place of governance in Europe. Still, at least the proposal exists, and France hasn't even deigned to respond to it or formulate its own version.

So what to do? First it needs to be repeated that a single currency with seventeen different public debts cannot work. The loss of monetary sovereignty has to be compensated by access to mutualized public debt and a low and predictable interest rate. It has to be understood that with a public debt around 100 percent of GDP, waves of speculation on interest rates have huge and devastating effects on public finances. Italy now has a primary budget surplus of 2.5 percent of GDP (i.e., taxes exceed public spending by 2.5 percent of GDP), and interest payments on the debt alone are plunging the country into deficits and a debt spiral. By way of comparison, the total budget for all higher education in France and in Italy is on the order of 0.5 percent of GDP.

Whatever the errors of the past − and errors there were − it makes no sense to impose such a cost on Italy, Spain, and Greece, and such an inability to invest in the future. No one can reform their country with such uncertainty hanging over their heads.

A political and fiscal union of the Eurozone is also the only way to equitably share sacrifice. One of the effects of this crisis has been the grand return of the wealth tax. There's nothing surprising about that: in Europe private wealth is now at levels unknown since the Belle Époque, while incomes are stagnating. In Spain, the wealth tax eliminated by Prime Minister José Luis Rodríguez Zapatero in 2008 was reintroduced in 2011. In Germany, the Social Democratic Party wants to re-create a general tax on wealth. In Italy, most of the new tax receipts raised by the government of Mario Monti come from an increase in tax on real estate and financial assets. Even the IMF, whose tax doctrine usually amounts to promoting VAT taxes, applauded.

The problem is that it's impossible to carry out this type of reform properly without European cooperation. And in particular without the automatic exchange of information on financial assets held abroad. That's how Italy found itself introducing a 0.5 percent tax on real estate (which cannot be shifted offshore) and only 0.1 percent on financial assets, even though the latter represent the bulk of the biggest wealth holdings.

On the one hand, the creditors are asking Greece to make its most fortunate citizens pay; but on the other hand we refuse to put in place the fiscal union that would make it possible to realize this objective, and instead we're pushing southern Europe to launch a vast selloff of public assets at low prices. When will we see some coherence and some courage?

Since late 2011, Italy had been led by a nonpartisan, technocratic government headed by former European commissioner Mario Monti. Installed in office after bond market turmoil and pressure from Eurozone leaders had forced Silvio Berlusconi's resignation as prime minister, the Monti government lasted only a year before Berlusconi announced his intention to run for prime minister again. In response, Monti called new elections to seek a mandate from voters.

Italy's general election took place on February 24–25, 2013. In the meantime, the Five Star Movement, a new populist and anti-euro party led by comedian turned politician Beppe Grillo, had become a major force in Italian politics.

The Italian Elections: Europe's Responsibility

February 26, 2013

From a French perspective, the incredible Berlusconi come-back in the Italian election campaign, the large populist vote more generally, and the political instability that the coming years seem to promise, appear hard to understand. There is, of course, an irreducible Italian and Berlusconian specificity. But it would be too easy to chalk it all up to Italian exoticism, unrelated to our own realities and our own responsibilities. France, too, has its surprising electoral tendencies, starting with the far-right Le Pen vote, which continues to astonish foreign observers.

The infatuation with comedian Beppe Grillo, who won over many left-wing voters by proposing both a minimum income and a referendum on exiting the Eurozone, with the support of intellectuals and writers like Dario Fo, is not without a certain resemblance to France's infatuation with the entertainer Coluche in late 1980 and early 1981, who was above 15 percent in presidential election polls and was supported by such public intellectuals as Pierre Bourdieu and Gilles Deleuze, before withdrawing from the race. In both cases we find the same distrust of political elites seen as careerists, and the lack of courage and clarity of their promises. Are we really sure this couldn't happen again in France?

But if the Italian election is important, it's above all because the growing distrust of Europe among Italians – until recently the most European of us all – is due in part to our own selfishness and timidity. The EU, and especially the leaders of its two main economic and political powers, Germany and France, bears an enormous responsibility for the catastrophic situation the Eurozone finds itself in today, which casts a growing shadow on the political climate in southern Europe. The spark could reignite at any moment in Greece or Spain, where a high-stakes vote on independence for Catalonia will take place in 2014.

It's often said that the ECB, the only strong federal EU institution, has succeeded in convincing financial markets that it will always be there to rescue the euro, and that this is what made it possible to exit the crisis. In reality, a central bank alone can't guarantee the sustainability of a monetary union. The best evidence is that Italy and Spain continue to pay interest rates much higher than Germany and France.

In 2012 Italy sharply cut spending and raised taxes, in par-ticular by creating a new tax on real estate wealth (as well as on financial assets, but at a rate eight times lower due to a lack of adequate European cooperation), so that at this point the country finds itself with a primary budget surplus: taxes exceed spending by 2.5 percent of GDP. The problem is that this policy has plunged the country into recession, but with-out allowing it to exit the debt spiral: interest on public debt exceeds 5 percent of GDP, so that the overall deficit – which is what matters for the size of the debt – is more than 2.5 per-cent of GDP. The sacrifices accepted by the public seem to be in vain.

Monti is the subject of adulation in the rest of Europe, but to the Italians all of this seems absurd. Unsurprisingly, Ber-lusconi proposes to refund the new tax, and Beppe Grillo proposes to exit the euro. To tell the truth, this is not a new situation for Italy, which has regularly found itself running large primary surpluses to deal with the weight of interest payments created by earlier deficits. Italy is the only G-8 coun-try that has been in a situation of a nearly balanced primary budget for the whole of the period 1970–2010 (on average, government spending has barely exceeded tax receipts). It's also the country whose debt has increased the most, because interest on debt exceeded 6 percent of GDP on average (versus 2 to 3 percent everywhere else).

What's new is that until now Italy could devalue its currency to get out of its difficult straits and restart the machine. With the euro, countries have given up their mon-etary sovereignty. In exchange, there needs to be a mutualized public debt, letting everyone benefit from low and predict-able interest rates. That would obviously require a common European vote on deficits, done in a transparent and democratic way, probably by bringing together members of the national parliaments' finance committees to create a real fiscal parliament of the Eurozone. If Germany and France don't finally get past their selfishness to propose such a solution, there's a strong risk that new political earthquakes will be triggered, more serious than the Italian vote.

For a European Wealth Tax

March 26, 2013

The Cyprus crisis illustrates some of the thorniest contradictions confronting financial globalization. What are they? Cyprus is an island of one million people, which joined the European Union in 2004 and the Eurozone in 2008. It has a hypertrophied banking sector, with balance sheets greater than eight times GDP and deposits reaching four times GDP. These are both Cypriot and foreign deposits – especially Russian – attracted by low taxes and uninquisitive local authorities.

We're told that these Russian deposits include enormous individual amounts, so one pictures oligarchs with assets in the tens of millions of euros. That's probably true, but not even approximate figures have ever been published by the European authorities or the IMF. The institutions themselves probably don't know much about the subject, and have never sought the means to make any progress on the issue, even though it's a central one. This opacity isn't facilitating a calm and rational solution to the conflict.

The problem of the day is that Cypriot banks, in effect, don't have that money anymore: it was invested in now-depreciated Greek bonds and real estate investments that were partly illusory. Quite naturally, the European authorities are reluctant to bail out banks without getting anything in return, especially if that ultimately means bailing out Russian millionaires.

After months of reflection, the members of the now famous troika (the European Commission, the ECB, and the IMF) got the disastrous idea to tax all bank deposits, practically at the same rate: 6.75 percent up to €100,000 and 9.9 percent beyond that. The slight progressivity shouldn't mislead: to most people, this means hitting ordinary savings accounts and oligarchs in the same way.

Faced with opposition, there's now talk of exempting deposits under €100,000 and taxing higher deposits more heavily. But it's still very vague (apparently things are moving toward a more bank-by-bank approach), and most important, the harm is done: small European depositors no longer know whether they can have confidence in the governing authorities.

According to the official version, this quasi 'flat tax' was adopted at the request of Cyprus's president, who wanted to tax small depositors heavily to avoid causing the biggest ones to flee. That's probably true in part (we'll never know: all the negotiations took place behind closed doors). The Cypriot crisis illustrates the drama of small countries under globalization, which, in order to save their own skins and find their niche, are often willing to resort to the most ruthless tax competition to attract the most disreputable capital.

But the excuse only holds in part: the flat tax was unanimously adopted by the Eurogroup. It's time that European governments learn to assume their responsibilities publicly. This crisis shows the necessity of establishing a genuine Eurozone fiscal parliament, so that these questions can finally be debated and decided democratically, in broad daylight.

This crisis also illustrates the big countries' inability to put in place the tools they need to manage financial crises effectively and distribute sacrifices and losses in a way that's fair and acceptable to all. The problem of the Cypriot wealth levy is the narrowness of its base (apparently all you had to do to escape it was to transfer your deposits into securities accounts or other untaxed assets) and its blatant, historically unique lack of progressivity.

By way of comparison, the rate of the French wealth tax in 2013 is 0 percent up to €1.3 million, 0.7 percent up to €2.6 million, and rises to 1.5 percent beyond €10 million. One can also find a number of historical examples of temporary and progressive capital levies. The 'national solidarity tax' instituted in 1945 included an exceptional double levy, on the current value of wealth holdings (at rates ranging from 0 to 20 percent for the highest fortunes) as well as on wealth accumulation that had taken place between 1940 and 1945 (at rates going up to 100 percent for the largest accumulations).

To levy this kind of tax, there obviously need to be individual declarations of wealth that include the assets held in various banks. Modern means facilitate this task: with automatic information transmission between countries, we could even have pre-filled-out declarations. But it's precisely this prospect of an international wealth tax that the troika, and especially the IMF, rejects, out of conservatism and ideology. Hence the idea for the flat tax, which can be levied at the level of individual banks, and which is profoundly unfair and inefficient. At least the Cypriot crisis has the virtue of putting this debate clearly out in the open.

Although France's revolutionary First Republic abolished s.
1794, it was reintroduced by Napoleon Bonaparte in 1802. N ...ntil
the short-lived Second Republic of 1848 was slavery permanently
abolished. Nearly 250,000 slaves were emancipated, mostly in the
French colonies of Guadeloupe, Martinique, and Réunion.

On May 10, 2001, the French National Assembly passed a law
sponsored by French Guiana deputy Christiane Taubira
recognizing the slave trade as a crime against humanity. The date
was subsequently designated an annual day of commemoration of
slavery and abolition. After winning election in 2012, François
Hollande appointed Taubira justice minister.

Slavery: Reparations Through Transparency

May 21, 2013

Can we envision financial reparations for the crimes committed during slavery? Decreeing that 'history cannot be the
object of a transaction,' François Hollande answered that
question in the negative on May 10, the day of commemoration of slavery's abolition. It's a deft phrase. But if you look
closer, the issue is more complex and it can't be pushed aside
so easily. Justice Minister Christiane Taubira, the architect of
the 2001 law that recognized the slave trade as a crime against
humanity and made May 10 a day of commemoration, was

right to adjust the administration's position the next day by mentioning the need to think about land policies and land redistribution for the benefit of descendants of slaves in the French Overseas Departments and Territories.

A few years ago, a commission charged with looking into the plundering of Jewish assets and determining the necessary reparations was finally able to carry out its investigations in France. Was that a 'transaction with history'? Just ten years ago, several countries in the former Soviet Union and eastern Europe chose to carry out property restitutions and compensations concerning events that had taken place there almost a century earlier. In the major French slave islands (Réunion in the Indian Ocean, Martinique and Guadeloupe in the Antilles, which comprise nearly two million inhabitants between them), the abolition of slavery happened in 1848, just a century and a half ago. Are we really sure that this slight difference in historical distance is enough to definitively close the debate?

It would be especially unjustified because legal exploitation actually continued far past the 1848 abolition, often into the late nineteenth and early twentieth centuries. In Réunion, slavery was immediately replaced by a decree obliging people of color to show a long-term work contract as a domestic or agricultural worker, with those failing to comply imprisoned as vagrants.

Recent debates have also reminded us of a little-known part of this story. In practice, abolition was often accompanied by very substantial financial reparations . . . to the slave owners. An extreme case is the United Kingdom. Immediately after the 1833 law abolishing slavery in the British Antilles, Mauritius, and the Cape Colony, the British Parliament had no qualms about passing a generous compensation law: £20 million (around 5 percent of British GDP at the time, on the order of €100 billion today) was paid out by tax-payers to some three thousand slave owners (the equivalent of more than €30 million each).

That improbable episode has given rise to a remarkable recent effort at transparency led by a team of researchers from University College London, who put online a complete list of the slave owners in question, with all the details about the sums received, the numbers of slaves involved, and so on (type 'Legacies of British Slave-ownership' into your search engine). That's how it was learned that a cousin of the current prime minister owes a good part of his current fortune to such compensation.

In France, a law passed in 1849 also paid planters and colonists compensation for the emancipation of their approxi-mately 250,000 slaves (mainly in Réunion, Martinique, and Guadeloupe). The sums appear to have been more limited than in the UK, but no equivalent effort at transparency has been carried out so far. France is also different in that the islands in question are still part of the nation, and inequalities between descendants of slaves and those of planters are still very visible.

As Christiane Taubira has noted, not without irony, land redistribution would be easier to carry out in French Guiana, where the state owns a significant share of the land, than in the Antilles, where a good part of the land still belongs to the slave masters' descendants. France is also known for an aston-ishing episode, the subject of the current complaint filed by the Representative Council of France's Black Associations (*Conseil représentatif des associations noires de France*, or CRAN). In 1825 France recognized the sovereignty of Haiti in exchange for the payment of 150 billion gold francs (the equivalent of 2 percent of French GDP at the time), to compensate the colonists whose fortunes had been built on slavery. The tribute came out to 90 billion francs in the end, but Haiti would be weighed down by a colossal external debt until the twentieth century, to 'repay' France.

It must be emphasized that CRAN (which is now suing the government-run financial institution that manages these funds) is not asking for individual reparations but rather payments that will make it possible to increase transparency on these issues, through research and museums (along the lines of the International Slavery Museum in Liverpool). The idea is to establish a commission charged with shedding light on all of these questions. A provision pointing in this direction was struck out of the 2001 bill by the majority at that time. It's time to reintroduce it.

A New Europe to Overcome
the Crisis

June 18, 2013

Five years after the financial crisis began, the United States has returned to growth. Japan looks set to do the same. Only Europe seems trapped in ongoing stagnation and distrust: the continent still hasn't regained its 2007 level of activity. The European debt crisis looks insurmountable, even though the level of public debt is lower than in the rest of the wealthy world.

The paradox doesn't stop there. Europe's social model is the best in the world, and there is every reason to unite to defend, improve, and promote it. Total wealth (real estate and financial assets net of all debts) held by Europeans is the highest in the world, far above the United States and Japan, very far ahead of China. Contrary to a stubborn myth, what Europeans own in the rest of the world is far greater than what the rest of the world owns in Europe.

So why, despite all its social, economic, and financial advantages, is the continent failing to overcome the crisis? Because we continue to be divided over small details, and because we're content to remain a political dwarf and a tax sieve. We're governed by small countries in exaggerated competition with one another (France and Germany will soon be minuscule on the scale of the world economy), and by institutions that are totally dysfunctional and inappropriate.

After the fall of the Berlin Wall and the shock of German unification, it took European leaders a few months to decide on creating the common currency. Five years after the onset of the most serious economic crisis since the 1930s, we're still waiting for the same kind of courage. Yet the problem is clear. A single currency with seventeen different public debts and twenty-seven different tax policies that are mainly trying to siphon tax receipts from their neighbors does not work. But to unify public debts and institute a budget and tax union, Europe's political architecture must be fundamentally revised.

The heart of the problem is the Council of Heads of State – and its extensions at the ministerial level (council of finance ministers, Eurogroup, etc.). We pretend that it can take the place of a sovereign parliamentary chamber, as if it were a chamber representing states, alongside the European Parliament representing citizens.

This fiction doesn't work and will never work, for a simple reason: a calm, public, and pluralistic parliamentary democracy can't be organized with a single representative per country. Such a body naturally leads to clashes of national self-interest and to collective impotence. This goes beyond individuals: 'Merkhollande' doesn't work any better than 'Merkozy.'

The council is useful for determining general rules and negotiating treaty changes. But to manage a real tax and budget union on a day-to-day basis, to have a sovereign vote on public deficit levels and adjust them to the trend of the business cycle (once you start mutualizing debts, you can't keep having everyone choose their own deficit level), to democratically determine the base and rates of the taxes that must be levied in common (starting with the corporate tax, which is now massively evaded by multinationals), we need a real budgetary parliament of the Eurozone.

The most natural solution would be to build on the basis of national parliaments – for example, by assembling deputies from the finance committees of the Bundestag, the French National Assembly, and so on, who could sit in session together one week per month to make decisions in common. Thus, each country would be represented by thirty or forty people, and not by just one. Votes would not amount to national confrontations: French Socialist Party deputies would frequently vote with their German counterparts, our right wing with theirs. Above all, debates would be public, with opposing views, and would result in a clear and distinct majority decision.

We would no longer have the façade of unanimity of the Council of Heads of State, whose members regularly announce at four in the morning that they've saved Europe, before people realize the next day that they themselves don't know what they decided on. The prize for irresponsibility undoubtedly goes to the decisions on Cyprus that were made unanimously by the Eurogroup and the European Commission, ECB, IMF troika, and which no one was willing to take responsibility for in the days that followed.

The problem is that the governments in place seem to be fond of this system. Ultimately there's a fairly broad consensus, ranging from free market Germans to French Socialists, that European political power should remain in the Council of Heads of State.

Why this timorousness? The official explanation is that the French public doesn't want federalism, and that it would be suicidal to launch into a treaty change. It's an odd argument: from the moment more than twenty years ago when we chose to share monetary sovereignty and set extremely picayune rules on public deficits (like the 0.5 percent threshold for structural deficits and the automatic penalties for noncompliance fixed by the treaty adopted last year), we've been de facto in a federal system.

The question is simple: Do we want to keep endlessly moving further into a technocratic federalism, or are we finally ready to bet on democratic federalism?

Can Growth Save Us?

September 24, 2013

Is it sensible to bet on a return to growth to solve our problems? Of course, 1 percent growth in production and national income is always preferable to 0 percent. But it's time to realize that that won't resolve most of the challenges that wealthy countries will have to deal with in the early twenty-first century.

Production can grow for two reasons: because of population growth and because of growth in per capita production, or productivity. Over the past three centuries, world production grew by 1.6 percent per year on average, of which 0.8 percent was through population growth and 0.8 percent through per capita production. That might seem tiny, but in reality it's a very rapid pace if continued over a long period. In fact, it corresponded to a tenfold growth of world population in three centuries, from roughly six hundred million people around 1700 to seven billion today. It seems unlikely that that pace of demographic growth will continue in the future. Population has already started declining in several European and Asian countries. According to United Nations forecasts, world population as a whole is expected to stabilize over the course of the century.

As for per capita production, it's entirely possible to imagine those past growth rates – 0.8 percent per year for the last three centuries – continuing into the future. I am not an adherent of the 'de-growth' perspective.* Technological innovation permitting nonmaterial, nonpolluting growth could very well continue indefinitely. But only if we come up with clean energy sources, which can't be taken for granted. In any case, the important point is that even if growth continues, it probably won't exceed 1 to 1.5 percent per year. The 4 or 5 percent growth rates seen in Europe during the postwar decades, the even higher rates in China today, represent purely transitory situations of countries catching up relative to others. No country, upon reaching the world technological frontier, has ever experienced sustained growth rates above 1 to 1.5 percent per year.

In these conditions, it's almost inevitable that growth in the twenty-first century will settle at a rate far lower than the rate of return to capital – that is, what wealth earns on average over the course of a year (in the form of rents, dividends, interest, profits, capital gains, etc.) as a percentage of its initial value. This rate of return is generally on the order of 4 to 5 percent per year (for example, if an apartment worth €100,000 has a rental value of €4,000 euros a year, the return is 4 percent), and can reach 7 to 8 percent per year for stocks and the biggest and most diversified wealth holdings.

But this inequality between the return to capital (r) and the growth of production (g), which can be noted $r > g$, automatically gives disproportionate weight to wealth that was constituted in the past, and leads mechanically to an extreme concentration of wealth. We've started to see signs of it in the last few decades, in the United States, of course, but also in

---

* The de-growth movement – established in Europe but less so in the United States – advocates for the shrinking of economies and a decrease in consumption. – *Trans.*

Europe and Japan, where reduced growth (especially demographic growth) is causing an unprecedented increase in the mass of wealth relative to income.

It's important to understand that there's no natural reason why the rate of return to capital should fall to the level of the growth rate. The simplest way to see this is to note that growth was practically zero for most of human history, while the return to capital was always clearly positive (typically 4–5 percent for landed wealth in traditional agricultural societies). From a strictly economic point of view, this poses no logical problem. Quite the contrary: the purer and more perfect the capital market (in the economist's sense), the greater the $r > g$ gap will be. And yet that leads to extreme inequality, incompatible with the meritocratic values on which our democratic societies are based.

A number of remedies are possible, ranging from the greatest international cooperation (automatic exchange of bank information, a progressive tax on capital) to the greatest national isolation. Inflation would help liquidate public debt, but would mainly hit modest wealth holdings, and is therefore not a sustainable response. Chinese-style capital controls, Russian-style authoritarian oligarchy, perpetual demographic growth as in America: each regional bloc has its solution. Europe's good fortune is its social model and its great wealth, which far exceeds all its debts. Provided that it radically revises its political institutions, which are now seriously dysfunctional, it has the means to go beyond growth and help democracy retake control of capitalism.

IMF: Still a Ways to Go!

October 22, 2013

So the IMF has started defending progressive taxation in its latest report. It even recommends a tax on private wealth to reduce public debt. What a good idea! Of course, such a change of tune might raise a smile. But let's try to understand what the IMF is and isn't proposing, where it's coming from and where it's going.

For decades, the IMF has done everything possible to undermine the very principle of progressive taxation. In every country where it's intervened, it has favored taxes on consumption (which are not progressive), or even a flat tax, a tax with the same rate on all incomes, from the lowest to the most astronomical. Everywhere, it has explained that applying higher rates to higher tax brackets was harmful for growth and should be abandoned. This claim made no sense from a historical point of view: growth has never been as strong as it was in the years 1950 to 1980, a period when tax progressivity was at a maximum, especially in the United States.

Even today, most IMF officials, who draw $300,000 to $400,000 a year and, naturally, are exempted from all taxes, remain molded by that ideology. They still explain in all good conscience that budget adjustments should happen mainly through increases in the VAT tax and cuts in social spending, and they still defend reforms (like deductions for notional interest on stocks) that aim in practice to gut the corporate tax. To say that the new report is causing some teeth gnashing in the IMF corridors, and that there's a long ways left to go in changing these mentalities, is putting it mildly. Nevertheless, with its reminder that a good part of the current American deficit could be eliminated by returning to 1980 levels of tax progressivity, the Washington institution is taking an important step in its own history.

The battle over progressive income taxes is far from over. And behind this clash, an even more important intellectual and political battle is taking shape: the fight over a progressive wealth tax. The IMF is right to emphasize that public debts in the rich countries, which look insurmountable today, ultimately aren't much compared to the mass of private wealth (financial and real estate) held by those same countries' households, especially in Europe. The rich world is rich; it's the governments that are poor. The solution envisaged by the IMF – that is, taxing private wealth to reduce public debt – has the virtue of lifting a taboo. It demonstrates the institution's disarray in dealing with the current crisis. The IMF was unable to foresee the 2008 crisis and now it realizes that the austerity strategy it supported has only prolonged the recession, and that at this rate it would take several decades to bring debts back to their 2007 levels.

Unfortunately we're still only halfway there. The problem is that the IMF isn't clearly committing to progressive capital taxes as a way forward. The report does mention the possibility of a tax focused on the biggest wealth holdings. But it mainly seems to favor a flat wealth-tax-type solution, which is deeply unattractive: taxing small- and medium-sized savings at the same rate as very big financial portfolios makes no sense, and can only lead to a rejection of this kind of policy. Besides, the European authorities and the IMF supported such a solution in the Cyprus crisis last spring, and we can all see how successful that was (the report contains no mea culpa on this point: the episode isn't even mentioned). Given the extreme concentration in the distribution of capital, tax rates on wealth must be strongly progressive, even more so than for income.

But such progressivity requires a high degree of inter- national financial transparency and cooperation between countries, which the IMF hardly mentions. That's especially regrettable because without a clearly formulated objective on taxes, the current talks on tax havens are likely to get bogged down. The goal of automatic transmission of bank informa- tion must be the ability to observe all financial and real estate assets held by a given individual in different countries, and to levy a progressive tax on individual net wealth.

Let's dream a little: What if the officials of the European Commission and the European finance ministries, instead of always being led around by the IMF (led around, to parrot the ultraliberal tax orthodoxy, only to make a subsequent U-turn), decided to take the initiative and put forward proposals? What if Europe's political leaders, starting with the French and Ger- man leaders, finally assumed their responsibilities?

Libération *has been a fixture of the French media landscape since its 1973 founding, but by the 1990s it was suffering the same ills as the rest of France's national press: declining sales and revenues amid competition from the Internet. These problems were only partially ameliorated by France's system of press subsidies, which primarily take the form of tax exemptions.*

With rumors of imminent bankruptcy swirling, Libé's journalists launched a one-day strike in February 2014 to protest reorganization plans championed by businessman Bruno Ledoux, one of the paper's major shareholders. Ledoux envisioned a reduction in editorial staff and a diversification into new lines of business to capitalize on the paper's iconic brand.

Libé : What Does It Mean to Be Free?

February 25, 2014

The crisis at *Libé* at least has the virtue of raising a vital question: What does it mean to be free when you're owned by a shareholder, and what's more, a shareholder who's full of his own power? What alternative forms of governance should we come up with in the twenty-first century to escape the dictatorship of the all-powerful owner and finally allow democratic and participatory control of capital and the means of production? This eternal question, which some thought closed after the fall of the Soviet anti-model, never really went away.

It's especially present in the newspaper industry, and the media in general, where there has recently been heightened interest in mixed property structures, taking the form of associations or foundations with the twin objectives of guaranteeing editorial independence and promoting innovative models of financing. In the current context of acute crisis for the media, which is threatened by frantic competition and an erosion of editorial staff, the whole model needs to be rethought (as the recent works of the French economist Julia Cagé have shown).

But the issue of alternative forms of capital ownership arises in all cultural and educational sectors, and on every continent. To my knowledge, no one has proposed transforming Harvard (whose endowment is bigger than the capital of the largest European banks) into a stock corporation. To take a more modest example, the statutes of the Paris School of Economics Foundation specify that the number of board seats held by its private charter members rises slightly according to their capital contributions, but always stays below the number held by public founders and scientific officials. And that's a good thing: the temptation to abuse one's power can strike nice university donors as well as generous newspaper shareholders, so it's best to be armed and ready.

In truth, this same problem of power sharing arises in every sector, both in services and industry, where a number of alternative governance models still exist. For example, German workers are much more involved in the management of their companies than in France, and by all accounts that doesn't prevent them from producing good cars (which a recent book by the economist Guillaume Duval offers a very timely reminder of).

At *Libé*, the question is especially pressing now. The main shareholder, Bruno Ledoux, started off by thundering con-temptuously that *Libé* 'owes its salvation to the accumulation of subsidies from the government.' He then explained on TV that he wanted 'to call as witness the whole French people, who are shelling out for these guys.' These unprecedentedly harsh words for the journalists of a paper that he claims to want to save might seem incredible. But they're consistent with the so-called plan unveiled the same day, aiming to monetize the *Libé* brand by getting rid of the journalists.

The violence of these words, the aggression of 'King Money,' who seems to think he can do anything and say any-thing, is a challenge to all of us, as citizens and as *Libé* readers. One can sometimes be disappointed by the content of the newspaper, but all you have to do is turn on the cable news channels, with their incessant flow of dumbed-down dis-patches, to remember that democracy can't function without the sense of perspective and reflection that the written word and the general news daily can provide.

Libé must live, and for that it is necessary to condemn the lies that are being spread around. No, the media do not live off public charity! A media outlet like *Libération* actually pays much more in taxes than it receives in aid: at the very most, we can say that it's subject to an overall tax rate that's a bit lower than the average rate for private economic activities.

Let's put the issue in a broader context. Our economic model involves placing roughly half the wealth produced each year in common, in the form of various taxes used to finance infrastructure, public services, and collective protec-tions, from which we all benefit. It's not a situation where there are payers on the one hand and receivers on the other: everyone pays and everyone receives. In some supposedly purely private sectors, revenues from sales are expected to cover all costs, yet obviously that doesn't stop them from benefiting from public infrastructure. In other sectors, like health or education, the revenues that service users actually contribute represent only a very small part of the costs. This choice was made to guarantee equality of access to those services, but also because over the course of history we've been convinced that the model of absolute competition between profit-maximizing producers isn't always the best one – far from it.

The cultural and media sectors are in an intermediate position. We cherish the independence and dynamism that competing producers provide, but we mistrust the all-powerful stockholder. To build a viable model, we should probably accept that private revenue, as a share of total financing, will also be in an intermediate position: much greater than in higher education, for instance, but clearly lower than in the cosmetics industry. And of course, we should rid the industry of the little rulers who afflict it.

In McCutcheon v. Federal Election Commission, *the U.S. Supreme Court struck down aggregate limits on individual contributions to federal candidates and political parties. The decision followed in the footsteps of the court's 2010* Citizens United *decision, prohibiting limits on independent campaign spending by outside groups.*

On Oligarchy in America

April 21, 2014

Will oligarchy, or plutocracy, be America's future? A recent Supreme Court decision striking down all limits on private funding for political campaigns has rekindled that fear. The hundreds of millions doled out by the hyper-Republican billionaire Koch brothers for TV ads and think tanks backing the farthest-right candidates have become the symbol of all-powerful wealth. The specter of a slide into hyper-inequality and a politics increasingly captured by the '1 percent' is animating political debates across the Atlantic like never before. It's been several years now since the Occupy Wall Street movement and its peculiar slogans ('We are the 99 percent') took Europe by surprise. Our continent is far more preoccupied – in part for good reason – with modernizing its welfare state, and the dysfunctions of its single currency. If President Obama could recently deem inequality 'the defining challenge of our time,' it's above all because inequality's rise has been incomparably more massive in the United States. First the country witnessed an unprecedented takeoff in super-manager salaries; now it's the growing concentration of wealth that looks set to become the main issue. The share of national wealth held by the richest 1 percent in America is approaching the dangerous heights seen in Ancien Régime or Belle Époque Europe. For a country founded in large part as an antithesis to Europe's patrimonial societies, it's a rude awakening.

Up to now, America has been sheltered by the ceaseless growth of its population and the dynamism of its universities and innovations. But that's no longer enough. Once already, in the early twentieth century, the rise of inequality spurred a vast national debate – it was the era of the Gilded Age, of Rockefeller and Gatsby. That's how the country ended up devising heavy progressive taxation on high incomes and the biggest inherited fortunes, with top marginal rates reaching or exceeding 70–80 percent for half a century.

Will we see a similar response from American democracy in the years and decades to come? As the Supreme Court's decision shows, the political battle is shaping up to be tough – but it can be won. The justices once tried to block the income tax in the nineteenth century and the minimum wage in the 1930s. They seem well on their way to reprising the same reactionary role today, not unlike the French Constitutional Council, which is increasingly willing to give the force of law to its conservative views on taxes, all in good conscience.

An additional problem arises from the fact that regulating patrimonial capitalism in the twenty-first century requires new tools and new forms of international cooperation. The United States alone represents nearly a quarter of world GDP. The country is big enough to take action – especially to trans-form its flat tax on real estate (which dates to the nineteenth century, like similar taxes in Europe, such as France's *taxe fon-cière*) into an annual progressive tax on individual net worth (which takes debts and financial assets into account). That would improve the situation for first-time homebuyers while reducing concentration at the top. The United States has also shown itself capable of staring down the Swiss banks to obtain the automatic transmission of information on its nationals' financial assets.

To go further, the European Union, acting with the United States, must finally play its part and develop a genuine international register of assets and securities. The opacity of finance and the growing concentration of wealth are challenges for the entire world.

According to the rankings published since 1987 by *Forbes,* the biggest fortunes grew at an average rate of 6–7 percent per year between 1987 and 2013, versus barely 2 percent for average wealth worldwide. The risk of a drift toward oligarchy exists on every continent.

In China, so far the authorities have opted to deal with the problem case by case, as in Russia: oligarchs are tolerated so long as they're docile toward the regime, and they're expropriated when they threaten political elites or when it looks like the public's tolerance is reaching its limit. But it seems as if the Chinese authorities are starting to realize the limits of such an approach, and debates on creating a property tax are already underway. The country's size (soon almost a quarter of world GDP) and its high degree of centralization (much greater than in the United States) would allow it to act effectively if necessary.

In this global landscape, the European Union (the third quarter of world GDP) obviously suffers from its political fragmentation. Yet given the financing needs of its social model, it's the region of the world that has the most to gain from taking action against the tax havens. In proposing to put this issue at the heart of a future Euro-American trade treaty, it would have every chance of being heard by an America beset by doubts about inequality.

The 2014 European Parliament elections were the first to be held since the start of the continent's sovereign debt crisis. In the intervening period, popular dissatisfaction with the EU had led to a sharp rise in support for Euroskeptic and antiausterity parties, and the upcoming vote was seen as a test of their newfound strength.

In addition, the 2014 vote was the first since the Lisbon Treaty took effect. The treaty required that the European Council 'tak[e] into account' the results of the EP elections in selecting a nominee for president of the European Commission. Although there was some dispute over how to interpret this provision, each of the major Pan-European parties put forward a candidate for EC president, and it was generally expected that the post would go to the winning party's nominee.

To the Polls, Citizens!

May 20, 2014

Next Sunday, Europe's citizens will be able to change Europe by bringing Martin Schulz, of Germany's Social Democratic Party, to the head of the European Commission. In any case, that's what the Socialist candidates proudly proclaim in their professions of faith, forgetting rather quickly that they're already in power in France. So are we really going to change Europe tomorrow?

It can be said that this election probably holds a greater potential for change and transformation than any preceding

European election. For the first time, the vote might have a direct impact on the choice of the EC president. If the Socialist lists come out clearly on top, the heads of state will have no other choice but to propose Martin Schulz for the European Parliament's approval. Conversely, if the right-wing and center-right lists clearly dominate, they'll appoint Jean-Claude Juncker. It's Schulz, a solid and sincere Social Democrat, against Juncker, the immovable former leader of Luxembourg, the tax haven nestled in the heart of Europe, who for years has blocked every attempt to put in place the automatic transmission of bank information. The choice is basically pretty simple, and there's ample reason to go out on Sunday, unless you have something really important to do.

And yet, to change Europe, much more will be needed than a vote for Schulz. The management of the crisis has had disastrous results: in 2013–14 growth has been practically zero in the Eurozone, while it has clearly returned in the United States and the United Kingdom. Why have we transformed a crisis of public debt, which was initially just as high across the Atlantic and the Channel, into a crisis of Eurozone distrust that seriously risks trapping us in a long stagnation? Because our common institutions are failing. To return to growth and social progress in Europe, they must be fundamentally rethought.

That's the idea of the Manifesto for a Euro Political Union, which has now been translated and published in six European languages (pouruneunionpolitiquedeleuro.eu). The central idea is simple. A single currency with eighteen different public debts on which markets can freely speculate, as well as eighteen different tax and social systems in unfettered competition with one another, does not work and will never work. The countries of the Eurozone have chosen to share their monetary sovereignty, and thus to give up the weapon of unilateral devaluation, but without giving themselves new joint economic, social, tax, and budget instruments. This is the worst of both worlds.

And whatever the goodwill of Martin Schulz, whatever majority he may have in the European Parliament, he will face the roadblock of the all-powerful Council of Heads of State. To put an end to the unanimity rule, we have to institute a real parliamentary chamber of the Eurozone, where each country could be represented by deputies from all political tendencies and not by a single person. Without that, the inertia will continue: the same inertia that resulted in our having to wait for American sanctions against Swiss banks in order to make some progress on financial transparency in Europe; the same inertia that constantly pushes us to cut corporate tax rates and to allow big multinationals to pay no taxes anywhere.

To illustrate the serious dysfunction of today's European institutions, one could also mention the lamentable tax on Cypriot deposits, approved unanimously in March 2013 in the opacity of the Eurogroup, before it turned out that no one was willing to defend it. If a new crisis happens on a larger scale we can expect the worst. To shout that public opinion doesn't like the existing Europe, and then conclude that nothing essential should be changed in the way Europe functions, is a shameful contradiction. The treaties are changed constantly, and will be again in the future. Rather than standing around waiting for future proposals from Angela Merkel, better to prepare for it now and propose a real democratization of Europe.

To change Europe, we will also have to face head-on the question of a future Euro-American trade treaty. The EU and United States represent half of global GDP. Their responsibilities, and the expectations of their publics, can't be reduced to trade liberalization. Through this treaty, using the European Parliament and national parliaments, we can impose exacting standards in the social, environmental, and tax realms. The EU and the United States have the necessary size to impose new rules on their companies and on tax havens: a consolidated tax base for corporate taxes, a global – or at least Euro-American – register of financial securities. In these moves, Martin Schulz can play a central role. So let's dream a little, and vote.

In late August 2014 a major escalation of the conflict in eastern Ukraine took place as Russia sent personnel and materiel across the border in what the Ukrainian government called a 'direct invasion by Russia of Ukraine.' The move was condemned by NATO and prompted an escalation of EU sanctions.

The Exorbitant Cost of Being a Small Country

September 8, 2014

So it took thousands of deaths in Ukraine and months of guilty hesitation for France to finally agree to a provisional suspension of arms deliveries to Russia. All that for some frigate sales that bring in barely more than a billion euros, an utterly derisory sum relative to the human and geopolitical stakes involved and the military danger those arms transfers represent. By way of comparison, we might recall that the U.S. criminal justice system just quietly fined BNP Paribas more than $9 billion. Imagine what would have been said if the French state had tried to make our leading national and European bank pay such a sum! These two figures, which seemingly have nothing to do with each other, are actually two sides of the same coin. In the new world economy, the cost of being a small country is becoming exorbitant: we find ourselves accepting things that are more and more unacceptable and contradictory to our values.

To pick up a few billion in exports, we're now willing to sell anything to anyone. We're willing to become a tax haven, to have oligarchs and multinationals paying less in taxes than the middle and working classes, to ally with rather unprogressive oil emirates just to get a few crumbs for our football teams. And conversely, we're subjected to the law of the big countries – the United States, as it happens – which use the weight of their justice systems to impose record fines and arbitrary decisions pretty much everywhere in the world, whether in France or in Argentina (whose debt repayments have now suddenly been called into question). Yet all European countries, including France and Germany (which was recently scandalized by the National Security Agency wiretapping affair), are increasingly going to find themselves in the position of being tiny countries, willing to sacrifice everything and endure anything. That's why, for a long time to come, political union will be the top priority for our time and our continent, in the name of our values and our European model of society.

Yet this union isn't getting anywhere. We may celebrate the fact that a Pole, former prime minister Donald Tusk, was just named European Council president and see it as a sign of success for the EU's eastward expansion. With a population of more than 500 million people and a GDP of more than €15 trillion, nearly a quarter of world GDP, the EU of twenty-eight countries has the means to impose decisions and sanctions. On Russia, notably, whose economic and financial weight is one-tenth the EU's, and which couldn't long withstand any determined action. Yet at the same time, this Polish president is also reminding us that Poland currently has no desire to enter the Eurozone, which represents the political and economic heart of Europe (nearly 350 million people and

€12 trillion in GDP), but which looks more and more like a failure in the eyes of the world, and to Europeans as well.

We have to look at the evidence: if we want to move toward political union, especially on tax, budget, and financial issues, it won't happen unless we build new democratic parliamentary institutions in a small number of countries of the Eurozone. With a Eurozone parliament and a finance minister who's responsible to it, we could vote in broad daylight on stimulus, a new common deficit, a common tax on companies and bank regulation, and create a political and democratic counterweight to the ECB, from which we can't expect everything. Once this strengthened union has shown its effectiveness and its ability to create political will and social progress, then the other countries in this union of twenty-eight will perhaps want to join the inner core. If we sit around and do nothing, things are not going to work themselves out on their own.

The French government, along with the Italian government and a few others, must now make proposals. It makes no sense to keep saying it's impossible to modify the treaties when in 2012 they were reformed in six months, and will be again. Although Germany will no doubt fear being put in the minority on the choice of a deficit level, it won't long be able to refuse a real proposal for stronger political union given that, obviously, it will have all its demographic weight reflected in the euro parliament. The French government won't be able to spend the next three years waiting for a recovery. François Hollande made an enormous mistake in 2012 in thinking that his strategy of breakneck deficit reduction would make possible a return to growth. It's time to admit it, and change it before it's too late.

In the fall of 2014, Hong Kong, which is governed as a Special Administrative Region of the People's Republic of China, was the scene of mass Occupy-style sit-in protests in opposition to Beijing's proposals for reforming the city's electoral system. At their peak, the protests drew more than one hundred thousand demonstrators.

Capital in Hong Kong?

November 3, 2014

According to the dictionary, *plutocracy* (from the Greek *ploutos*, 'wealth,' and *kratos*, 'power') is a system of government where money is the basis of power. To analyze the system that the Chinese Communist Party is currently trying to set up in Hong Kong, one is tempted to invent a new word: *plutocommunism*. Formally free elections are allowed, but only between two or three candidates, who must first be approved by a nominating committee appointed by Beijing and monopolized by Hong Kong business elites and various pro-China oligarchs.

Essentially it's a remarkable mix between the Communist logic of single-party rule (in East Germany there were elections, but only between candidates loyal to the existing regime) and the aristocratic and unequal suffrage traditions of Europe (until 1997 the governor of Hong Kong was appointed by the British monarch and democracy was indirect, based on committees dominated by economic elites). In the United Kingdom, as in France, between 1815 and 1848 only a small percentage of the population had the right to vote: those who paid enough taxes. (It's a bit like if, in today's France, only taxpayers subject to the ISF, the wealth tax, could vote.) Without going quite that far, China seems tempted by a similar path, but with a single all-powerful party to guide the whole thing.

How can such a system be justified, and does it have a future? It's putting it mildly to say that the Chinese Communists are not very convinced by the Western-style model of electoral multiparty democracy based on competition at every stage: among parties, among candidates, and perhaps even more important, among territories. For Beijing, the most important thing is the political unity of China's vast territory: that's the precondition for harmonious economic and social development, led by the Chinese Communist Party, the guarantor of the general and long-term interest. Indeed, compared to other emerging countries, especially India, China's success can be explained in part by political centralization and the ability of public authorities to finance collective infrastructure, mixed enterprises, and investments in education and health, which are indispensable for development.

Despite privatization, public capital still represents between 30 and 40 percent of China's national capital, compared to roughly a quarter in Europe during the postwar decades. The share is practically zero in most rich countries today (public assets barely exceed public debt), even negative in certain cases (where the public debt is larger, as in Italy), even as private capital, expressed in years of annual GDP, has returned to the peak levels of the pre-World War I era. From Beijing's perspective, the Chinese model seems better able to regulate capitalism and avoid the immiseration of public power. The feeling is reinforced by the gridlock of American politics and the impression that the European Union is going through an intractable slump, with a territory fragmented among twenty-eight small nation-states in frantic competition with each other, bogged down by public debt and totally dysfunctional common institutions, incapable of modernizing their social model and embracing the future.

However, even within the Chinese Communist Party there is a sense that China's current model, based on political closure and a struggle against corruption to limit the degree of inequality, won't be able to hang on forever. The growing influence of private fortunes in the National People's Congress is objectively rather worrying. In Beijing, what's feared more than anything is a Russian-style evolution, with mounting capital flight and a pillaging of the country from the outside, by oligarchs comfortably ensconced overseas. More and more, people are talking about introducing progressive taxes on inheritance and property. Indeed, in absolute terms, China's government has sufficient leverage to put in place a system for automatically transmitting banking information, a register of financial securities, and the capital controls needed to carry out such a policy.

The problem is that a good part of the political elite of China doesn't have much to gain from transparency on wealth, from progressive taxation, or the rule of law. And those who are ready to give up their privileges for the common good seem to think that the country's unity would be irremediably threatened by the emergence of political democracy, which would go hand in hand with the advent of economic democracy and tax and financial transparency. One thing is sure: these contradictions will give rise to a unique path that will be decisive for China, as well as the rest of the world. The struggles now underway in Hong Kong are a decisive step along that path.

Capital According to Carlos Fuentes

December 1, 2014

In 1865 Karl Marx said it was by reading Balzac that he learned the most about capitalism and the power of money. In *Destiny and Desire*, a magnificent epic published in 2008, a few years before his death, Carlos Fuentes painted a revealing portrait of Mexican capitalism and the social and economic violence of a country on the road to becoming the 'narco-nation' of today's headlines. The novel introduces us to colorful characters, with a president, puffed up by Coca-Cola PR, who in the end is merely a tenant of the eternal power of capital, embodied by an all-powerful billionaire bearing a strong resemblance to the telecommunications magnate Carlos Slim, the world's richest person.

Two young men wander between resignation, sex, and revolution. They will end up murdered by an ambitious beauty who wants their inheritance, and doesn't need the help of Balzac's expert criminal Vautrin to commit her infamy — proof, if any exists, that violence has gone up a notch since 1820. The transmission of wealth, object of all desires for those outside the privileged family circle, and at the same time personality-destroying for those within it, is at the heart of the novelist's meditation.

Here and there, we also see the harmful influence of the gringos, those North Americans who own '30% of Mexican territory' and its capital, and make inequality a little more intolerable still. Indeed, relations of property are always complex relations, hard to arrange peaceably even in the framework of a single political community: it's never simple to pay rent to one's landlord and amicably agree on the institutional details of this relationship and its perpetuation. But when it's a whole country paying rents and dividends to another country, it becomes frankly painful. Endless political cycles often follow, alternating between phases of triumphant ultraliberalism, authoritarianism, and the brief periods of chaotic expropriation that have always undermined the development of Latin America.

And yet, social and democratic progress remains possible on the continent. Further south, in Brazil, Dilma Rousseff was just reelected, barely, thanks to the vote of the poorer regions and the most disadvantaged social groups, which, despite the disappointments and reversals of the Workers' Party (in power since the election of Luiz Inácio Lula da Silva in 2002), are still very attached to the social advances they've benefited from, and which they fear seeing undermined by the return of the 'Right' (actually the Social Democratic Party, since in Latin America almost everyone says they're on the left, provided it's not too costly for the elites). Indeed, the social investment strategy undertaken by Lula and Rousseff, with the creation of the *bolsa familia* (a sort of family benefit reserved for the poorest), and even more so the increase in the minimum wage, have made possible a significant reduction in poverty over the last fifteen years. Today these fragile social rights are threatened by international forces that weigh heavily on the Brazilian economy, pushing it toward recession (the drop in raw materials prices, especially oil, the vagaries of U.S. monetary policy, Europe's austerity), and even more so by the immense inequality that undermines the country.

Here we find the weight of history's curse that Carlos

Fuentes speaks of. Brazil was the last country to abolish slavery, in 1888, at a time when slaves were nearly a third of the population, and nothing has really been done by the wealth-holding classes to overturn this heavy legacy of inequality. The quality of public services, and of the primary and secondary education open to the masses, remains low. The Brazilian tax system is heavily regressive, and finances public spending that is often just as much so. The working classes pay very heavy indirect taxes, with rates on electricity rising to 30 percent, while large inheritances are taxed at the risible rate of 4 percent. Public universities are free, but benefit only a small privileged minority. Timid mechanisms of preferential access to university for the working classes and black and mixed-race populations were put in place under Lula (with endless debates over the problems raised by racial self-classification in the census and administrative documents), but their presence in the lecture halls remains negligible. A good deal more struggle will be needed to shatter the curse of history and show that political will can overcome both good luck and bad.

*In November 2014, an international consortium of journalists
published a trove of papers documenting how, for years,
Luxembourg's tax authorities had crafted secret rulings tailored to
allow multinational companies to avoid foreign tax liabilities by
rerouting profits through subsidiaries in Luxembourg. These 'LuxLeaks'
revelations were made public just two weeks after the country's
longtime prime minister, Jean-Claude Juncker, assumed the post of
European Commission president. Following an uproar, the European
Parliament held a censure vote, which Juncker easily survived.*

2015: What Shocks Can Get Europe Moving?

December 29, 2014

The saddest thing about the European crisis is the determin-
ation of today's leaders to present their policies as the only
ones possible, and the fear they feel when any political shock
looks likely to disturb this happy equilibrium.

The prize for cynicism surely goes to Jean-Claude Juncker,
who's been calmly explaining to a dumbstruck Europe in the
wake of the LuxLeaks revelations that as Luxembourg's
prime minister he had no choice but to siphon off his neighbors' tax bases: The manufacturing industry was declining,
you see, so a new development strategy had to be found for
my country; what could I do but become one of the worst tax

havens on the planet? Those neighbors, who've also been struggling with deindustrialization for decades, will appreciate that.

Apologies are no longer enough. It's time to recognize that Europe's institutions themselves are the problem, and that only a democratic reconstruction of Europe will make it possible to carry out policies for social progress. Concretely, if we really want to prevent new LuxLeaks scandals from happening, we'll have to end the rule of unanimity for tax issues and make all decisions about taxing big companies (and ideally the highest incomes and biggest fortunes) according to majority rule. And if Luxembourg and other countries refuse, that shouldn't prevent countries wishing to do so from forming a core group to move ahead along that path, and to take any necessary sanctions against those who want to keep living off financial secrecy.

The prize for amnesia goes to Germany, with France a loyal second. In 1945 the two countries had public debts greater than 200 percent of GDP. By 1950, debt had fallen to less than 30 percent. What happened – did we suddenly run budget surpluses big enough to pay off such a debt? Obviously not: it was by inflation and repudiation, pure and simple, that Germany and France got rid of their debt in the previous century. Had they patiently tried to run surpluses of 1 or 2 percent of GDP a year, the debt would still be with us today, and it would have been much harder for postwar governments to invest in growth. Yet since 2010–11, those two countries have been explaining to southern Europe that their public debts will have to be paid back to the last euro. This is a shortsighted selfishness, for the new fiscal treaty adopted in 2012 under German and French pressure, which orchestrates austerity in Europe (with excessively rapid deficits reduction and a system

of totally ineffective automatic sanctions), has led to a generalized recession in the Eurozone. Meanwhile, economies
everywhere else have started recovering, both in the United
States and in the EU countries outside the Eurozone.

Of these two, the prize for hypocrisy, without contest,
goes to French leaders, who spend their time blaming every
mistake on Germany, even though the responsibility is clearly
shared. The new fiscal treaty, negotiated by the last government and ratified by the new one, couldn't have been adopted
without France, which, like Germany, made the selfish choice
vis-à-vis southern Europe: Since we pay a very low interest
rate, why share it? In truth, a single currency can't function
with eighteen different public debts and eighteen different
interest rates on which financial markets can freely speculate.
There needs to be massive investment in training, innovation,
and green technologies. We're doing exactly the opposite:
right now, Italy devotes nearly 6 percent of GDP to paying
interest on its debt and invests barely 1 percent of GDP in all
of its universities.

So what shocks could cause the ground to shift in 2015?
There are basically three possibilities: a new financial crisis, a
political shock coming from the left, or even a political shock
from the right. European leaders should have the intelligence
to see that the second possibility is by far the best: the political movements that are now prospering on the far left, like
Podemos in Spain or Syriza in Greece, are fundamentally
internationalist and pro-European. Rather than rejecting
them, we should work with them to formulate the outlines of
a democratic reconstruction of the EU. Without that, there's
a real risk that we'll find ourselves with an altogether more
worrying shock, coming from the right: given the French
voting system, it's entirely possible that the far-right Front

National will win some regions in the December 2015 regional elections. And since this is the season for New Year's wishes, we might also hope for the impossible. At this point, François Hollande would do well to recognize his mistakes from 2012, reach his hand out to southern Europe, and finally formulate some bold proposals for our continent.

*Formed in 2004, the Coalition of the Radical Left, or Syriza, was
initially a marginal party of the Greek Far Left. But it was
catapulted into prominence during the Greek economic crisis, and by
the 2012 elections it had grown to become the country's second-largest
party. Its sweeping victory in 2015, under the charismatic leadership
of Alexis Tsipras, was greeted with unease in European capitals and
euphoria within the European Left. Syriza called for an end to the
austerity policies demanded by the European 'troika' of economic
institutions under the terms of Greece's bailout, and said it was
prepared to challenge the Eurozone status quo even at the cost of a
serious confrontation with Europe's leaders.*

Spreading the Democratic Revolution
to the Rest of Europe

January 26, 2015

The electoral triumph of Syriza in Greece may be on the verge
of overturning the European status quo and putting an end to
the austerity undermining our continent and its youth. Especially since the Spanish elections scheduled for late 2015 may
produce a similar result, with the rise of Podemos. But in order
for this democratic revolution from the south to really change
the course of things, the center-left parties now in power in
France and Italy need to take a constructive attitude, recognizing their share of responsibility for the current situation.

In concrete terms, they should seize the moment to say loud and clear that the fiscal treaty adopted in 2012 has failed, and put new proposals on the table for a genuine democratic reconstruction of the Eurozone. Within the framework of current European institutions, hemmed in by rigid criteria on deficits and the rule of unanimity on taxes, it is simply impossible to carry out policies for social progress. It's not enough to complain about Berlin or Brussels: new rules have to be proposed.

Let's be clear: as long as we share the same currency, it's entirely justified to coordinate the level of deficits, as well as the overall orientation of our economic and social policies. But simply put, these common choices must be made in a democratic way, in broad daylight, following a public and pluralistic debate, and not by applying mechanical rules and automatic sanctions which, since 2011–12, have led to excessively rapid deficit reduction and a generalized recession in the Eurozone. The result has been an explosion of unemployment, which fell everywhere else (in the United States as well as the European countries outside the Eurozone), and public debts have increased, the opposite of the proclaimed objective.

The choice of deficit and public investment levels is a political decision that has to adapt quickly to the economic situation. It must be made democratically, within the framework of a Eurozone parliament in which each national parliament would be represented in proportion to the population of each country, neither more nor less. With such a system, we would have had less austerity, more growth, and lower unemployment. This new system of democratic governance would also make it possible to take up proposals for mutualizing public debts above 60 percent of GDP (in order to share the same interest rate and prevent future crises), and establishing a unified corporate tax for the Eurozone (the only way to put an end to tax dumping).

Unfortunately, the risk now is that the French and Italian governments will be content to treat Greece as a specific case, accepting a slight debt restructuring without fundamentally calling into question the organization of the Eurozone. Why? Because they've spent a lot of time explaining to their citizenry that the 2012 fiscal treaty is working, and they're afraid of reversing themselves now. So they'll explain that changing the treaties would be too complicated, even though rewriting them in 2012 took six months, and there's obviously no reason why emergency measures can't be taken while we wait for new rules to be instituted. It would be better to admit mistakes while there's still time rather than wait for new political shocks from the extreme right. If France and Italy now extend a hand to Greece and Spain and propose a real democratic reconstruction of the Eurozone, Germany will have to accept a compromise. It's the absence of proposals and prospects that's undermining Europe's debate.

Everything will also depend on the attitude of the Spanish Socialists, currently in opposition. Although they've been less crushed and discredited than their Greek counterparts, they must accept that they'll have a lot of trouble winning the next elections if they do not ally with Podemos, which may even come in first, according to the latest polls. So be it: the emergence of new political parties is sometimes necessary; what counts is the action plan that will come out of all this.

And above all, let's not imagine that the new ECB bond-buying plan will be enough to solve the problem. A single currency with eighteen public debts and eighteen different interest rates is fundamentally unstable. The ECB is trying to do its job, but to restart European growth and inflation there has to be a fiscal stimulus. Without that, the fear is that the billions of euros printed by the ECB will yield bubbles in certain assets, but not an increase in consumer-price inflation. The priority in Europe should now be investment in innovation and training. For that, there will have to be a strengthened political and fiscal union for the Eurozone, with majority decisions made in a genuinely democratic parliament. We can't ask everything of the central bank.

The Double Hardship of the Working Class

March 23, 2015

Why is the working class turning away from mainstream parties more or less everywhere, and especially from the center-left parties that claim to be their defenders? Quite simply, because the latter have not been defending them for a long time. Over the last few decades the working class has endured a double hardship, first economic and secondly political. Economic changes have been unfavorable to the most disadvantaged social groups in the developed countries: the end of the exceptional growth of the postwar decades, deindustrialization, the rise of emerging countries, the destruction of low- and medium-skilled jobs in the Global North. By contrast, those groups that are best equipped with financial and cultural capital have been able to benefit fully from globalization. The second problem is that political shifts have only made these trends worse. One might have imagined that public institutions and social welfare systems – policymaking overall – would adapt to the new situation by asking more from its main beneficiaries in order to devote more to the most affected groups. But the opposite has occurred.

Partly due to intensified competition between countries, national governments have focused more and more on the most mobile taxpayers (highly skilled and globalized workers, owners of capital) at the expense of groups perceived as captive (the working and middle classes). This pertains to a whole set of social policies and public services: investing in high-speed rail rather than commuter trains, elite educational institutions rather than ordinary public schools and universities, and so on. And of course it also pertains to how it's all financed. Since the 1980s, the progressivity of tax systems has been sharply reduced: rates that apply to the highest incomes were massively lowered, while indirect taxes hitting those of the most modest means were gradually increased.

Deregulating finance and liberalizing capital flows without asking anything in return has only worsened these trends.

European institutions as a whole, which have moved toward the principle of ever purer and more perfect competition between territories and countries, without a common tax and social base, have also reinforced these trends. We see it very clearly for the corporate tax: its rate has been cut in half in Europe since the 1980s. And it must be remembered that the biggest companies often escape the official tax, as the recent LuxLeaks scandal revealed. In practice, small- and medium-sized businesses find themselves paying rates far higher than those paid by multinationals headquartered in the big cities. More taxes, fewer public services: it's not surprising that the groups affected feel abandoned. This feeling of abandonment fuels the Far Right vote and the growth of Far Right parties, both inside and outside the Eurozone (as in Sweden). So what to do?

First, recognize that without radical social and democratic reconstruction, European integration will become more and more indefensible in the eyes of the working classes. From this point of view, the recent report of the 'Four Presidents' (European Commission, European Council, Eurogroup, and ECB) on the future of the Eurozone makes for particularly depressing reading. The general idea is that we already know the 'structural reforms' (fewer rigidities in labor and goods markets) that can fix everything, and all we have to do is find a way to impose them. The diagnosis is absurd: if unemployment has skyrocketed in recent years while it's fallen in the United States, it's chiefly because the latter has shown more fiscal flexibility and primed the pump.

What's immobilizing Europe is mainly its antidemocratic straitjackets: the rigidity of the budget criteria, the rule of unanimity on tax questions. And above all, the lack of investment in the future. An emblematic example: the Erasmus Program,★ which at least exists, is nevertheless ridiculously underfinanced (€2 billion per year versus €200 billion spent devoted to interest on debt), at a time when Europe should be massively investing in innovation, in youth, in its universities. If we don't reach a compromise to reconstruct Europe, the risk of an explosion is real. On Greece, certain leaders are clearly trying to push the country toward the exit: everyone is perfectly aware that the 2012 agreements can't be implemented (Greece is not going to repay 4 percent of its GDP in primary surpluses for decades), yet any renegotiation is refused. On all these issues, the total absence of any French proposals is becoming deafening. We can't wait with our arms crossed until France's regional elections in December, and the Far Right's arrival in power.

★ An EU-sponsored student exchange program established in the late 1980s, enrolling hundreds of thousands of students annually. – *Trans.*

Must Debts Always Be Paid Back?

April 20, 2015

For some, it's simple: debts must always be paid back. There's no alternative to repentance, especially when it's engraved in the marble of the European treaties. But a quick look at the history of public debt, a fascinating and unjustly neglected subject, shows that things are much more complicated.

First, the good news: in the past we find public debts even larger than those seen today, and we've always managed to overcome them, using a great variety of methods. We can distinguish, on the one hand, the slow method, which aims at patiently accumulating budget surpluses so that little by little the interest and then the principal of the debts are repaid; and on the other hand, a series of methods aiming to accelerate the process: inflation, exceptional taxes, cancellations pure and simple.

A particularly interesting case is that of Germany and France, which in 1945 found themselves with public debts of around two years' worth (200 percent) of GDP, levels even higher than Greece or Italy today. By the early 1950s those debts had fallen to less than 30 percent of GDP. Obviously, such a swift reduction wouldn't have been possible through accumulating budget surpluses. On the contrary, the two countries used the whole panoply of fast methods. Inflation, which was very high on both sides of the Rhine between 1945 and 1950, played the central role. At the time of the Liberation, France also instituted an exceptional tax on private capital, reaching 25 percent on the largest wealth holdings and even 100 percent on the biggest accumulations that had taken place between 1940 and 1945. Both countries also used various forms of 'debt restructuring,' the technical term used by financiers for simply canceling all or part of a debt (the more prosaic term *haircut* is also used). As, for example, in the famous London Accords of 1953, where the bulk of Germany's foreign debt was canceled. It was these fast methods of debt reduction – especially inflation – that allowed France and Germany to launch into reconstruction and postwar growth without the burden of debt. That's also how the two countries were able to invest in public infrastructure, education, and development in the 1950s and '60s. And it's those same two countries that are now explaining to southern Europe that public debts must always be repaid, down to the last euro, without inflation and without exceptional measures.

Currently Greece is reported to be running a slight budget surplus: the Greeks pay a bit more in taxes than they receive in public spending. According to the 2012 European agreements, Greece is expected to run an enormous surplus of 4 percent of GDP for decades, in order to pay back its debts. This is an absurd strategy that France and Germany, fortunately, never applied to themselves.

Germany obviously bears a heavy responsibility for this extraordinary historical amnesia. But these decisions could never have been adopted if France had opposed them. Successive French governments of the Right and now the Left have shown themselves incapable of taking stock of the situation and proposing a genuine democratic reconstruction of Europe.

Through their shortsighted selfishness, Germany and France are mistreating southern Europe, and at the same time they're mistreating themselves. With public debts nearing

100 percent of GDP, nonexistent inflation, and low growth, these two countries will also take decades to regain the capacity to act and invest in the future. The most absurd thing is that the European debts of 2015 are for the most part internal debts, as were those of 1945. Cross holdings between countries have certainly reached unprecedented levels: French banks hold a share of German and Italian debts, German and Italian financial institutions own a good part of France's debts, and so on. But if we consider the Eurozone in its entirety, we own ourselves. What's more: the financial assets we hold outside the Eurozone are greater than those held in the Eurozone by the rest of the world.

Rather than paying our debt back to ourselves for decades, all we have to do is organize things differently.

Secularism and Inequality: The French Hypocrisy

June 15, 2015

France often presents itself as a model of equality and religious neutrality. The reality, when it comes to jobs for example, is more complex and sometimes disturbing.

When it comes to religion, as in many other domains, every country likes to locate itself in a grand national narrative, which may be needed to give meaning to our collective destiny, but which too often serves to mask our hypocrisies. On religion, then, France likes to present itself as a model of neutrality, tolerance, and respect for different beliefs, without privileging any one of them: you won't see a president here swearing an oath on the Bible!

The truth is more complex. The religious controversy was brought to a close in this country through a massive assumption of public responsibility for Catholic schools, to a degree found in practically no other country. We're also the only country that chose to close the schools one day per week (Thursday from 1882 to 1972, then Wednesday) for catechism, a day that's only just been reintegrated – partially – into the normal school week. This awkward inheritance has left some monumental legacies and ambiguities. For example, already existing private Catholic schools are substantially financed by the taxpayer, but the conditions for opening new private schools belonging to other faiths have never been clarified, creating severe tensions around requests today for Muslim confessional schools. Likewise, houses of worship are not officially subsidized, except when it comes to buildings constructed before the church–state separation law of 1905.

And too bad if the map of religious observance has changed since then, and if mosques now find themselves housed in basements. The recent incident of the Muslim schoolgirls sent home because their skirts were too long has also shown where the law banning conspicuous religious symbols can lead. How can one be allowed to express any belief through one's clothing and appearance – for example with very short skirts, pleated skirts, dyed hair, rock-and-roll or revolutionary t-shirts – except one's religious beliefs?

Truly, apart from total face-covering (which prevents you from being identified), and certain parts of the body left too uncovered (an immodesty that would threaten public order, it seems), it would probably be wise to leave the choice of attire and adornment up to the individual. Secularism (*laïcité*) could then be about treating religion as a belief like any other, neither more nor less. An opinion, or rather a belief, that one may caricature like any other, that one may mock, of course, but that one also has the right to express, through language as well as dress.

But the most glaring French hypocrisy is probably our refusal to recognize the job discrimination endured by young people of Muslim origin or faith. A series of studies, carried out by Marie-Anne Valfort and others, has provided chilling evidence. The procedure is simple: fake CVs are sent to employers in response to thousands of job advertisements, while randomly varying the names and the CV details, and the response rate is observed. The results are depressing. When the name sounds Muslim, and above all when the candidate is male, response rates fall massively. Even worse: having the best educational credentials, completing the best possible internships, etc., has practically no effect on the response rates faced by young men of Muslim origin. In other words, discrimination is even greater for those who've met all the official requirements for success, who've satisfied every condition . . . except conditions they can't change.

The novelty of the study comes from its use of thousands of representative job advertisements from small- and medium-sized firms (for example, accounting jobs). Which probably explains why the results are far more negative – and unfortunately more convincing – than those obtained from the small number of very large firms that have volunteered to be studied in the past. What should be done, then? First of all, we need to become conscious of the magnitude of our collective hypocrisy, and give maximum publicity to these kinds of studies. Next, come up with new responses. Anonymous CVs, applied systematically to all hiring processes, perhaps aren't the miracle solution once hoped (it's a bit like combatting sexism in the workplace by preventing spontaneous encounters between the sexes).

But this approach shouldn't be totally dismissed. We could imagine systematically performing these kinds of random CV submissions, giving rise to exemplary penalties and court actions. More generally, all necessary resources must be devoted to enforcing the law and punishing discrimination. Grand national narratives and the prevailing conservatism shouldn't lead to a failure of imagination.

For an Open Europe

September 7, 2015

The drama of the refugees is an opportunity for Europeans to restart the continent's economy. Germany's attitude makes it a model to emulate.

However belated, the upsurge of solidarity toward the refugees seen these past weeks is at least reminding Europeans and the world of a fundamental reality. Our continent can and must become a major place of immigration in the twenty-first century. Everything points in this direction: the self-destructive aging of Europe's population makes it an imperative, its social model makes it possible, and Africa's demographic explosion (combined with global warming) will increasingly require it. All of this is well known. What's somewhat less understood is that before the financial crisis, Europe was on the way to becoming the most open region of the world in terms of migration flows. It was the crisis that began in the United States in 2007–8, which Europe still hasn't managed to move past due to the wrong policies, that led to the rise of unemployment and xenophobia and a brutal closing of the borders – and all while the international context (the Arab Spring, the surge of refugees) justified a further opening.

Let's step back. The European Union has a population of nearly 510 million in 2015, compared to roughly 485 million in 1995 (holding its borders constant). This population growth of 25 million in twenty years is hardly exceptional in itself (barely 0.2 percent growth annually, versus 1.2 percent for the world population as a whole over the same period). But the important point is that three-quarters of this growth is due to migration (more than 15 million). Thus, between 2000 and 2010, the European Union absorbed a flow of immigration (net of emigration) of roughly 1 million people per year – a level equivalent to the United States, and into a far more culturally and geographically diverse area (Islam remains marginal in the U.S.). In that era not too long ago when our continent was (relatively) welcoming, unemployment in Europe was falling, at least up until 2007–8. The paradox is that the United States, thanks to its pragmatism and its fiscal and monetary flexibility, recovered very quickly from the crisis it itself had triggered. It rapidly returned to growth (its 2015 GDP is 10 percent higher than in 2007), and immigration held steady at around 1 million people per year. But Europe, mired in sterile posturing and division, still hasn't regained its pre-crisis level of activity, resulting in rising unemployment and a closing of the borders. Immigration brutally declined from 1 million per year between 2000 and 2010 to less than 400,000 per year between 2010 and 2015.

What should be done? The drama of the refugees could be the occasion for Europeans to put their bickering and navel-gazing behind them. By opening up to the world, by restarting the economy and investment (housing, schools, infrastructure), by fending off deflationary risks, the European Union could absolutely return to its pre-crisis immigration levels. From that point of view, the openness shown by Germany is excellent news for those who've been worrying about a moldering, aging Europe. Of course, it could be asserted that Germany has little choice, given its very low birth rate. According to the latest UN projections, which assume an immigration rate twice as high in Germany as in France in the coming decades, Germany's population will nevertheless fall from 81 million to 63 million between now and the end of the century, while France's will rise from 64 to 76 million.

It might also be recalled that Germany's economic growth is due in part to a gigantic trade surplus, which by definition can't be extended to all of Europe (because no one on the planet could absorb such a volume of exports). But that growth is also explained by the efficiency of Germany's industrial model, which is based in part on a very high degree of involvement by workers and their representatives (with half the seats on the board of directors) – an example we would do well to learn from.

Most importantly, the openness to the world that Germany has shown sends a strong message to the EU members of the former Eastern Europe, who want neither more children nor more immigrants and whose combined populations, according to the UN, are expected to fall from 95 million today to little more than 55 million between now and the century's end. France should celebrate this German attitude and seize the opportunity to see an open and positive vision toward refugees, migrants, and the world carry the day.

Capital in South Africa

October 5, 2015

Just over twenty years after the end of apartheid and the first free elections (in 1994), South Africa is pondering the question of inequality more than ever. The Marikana massacre, where thirty-four miners, on strike for higher wages, were shot by police in August 2012, continues to weigh on many minds. The ANC (African National Congress), which has held power without interruption since the start of the democratic transition, has established equality of fundamental rights: the right to vote, the right of internal movement, and (in principle) the right to enter any profession. But this formal equality has not reduced the vast inequality in living standards and substantive rights: the right to a job and a decent wage, the right to a good education, the right to acquire property, and the right to genuine economic and political democracy. The country has developed, the population has risen sharply (30 million in 1980, 55 million today), but the promise of equality has not been realized.

According to the latest available figures, the wealthiest 10 percent control about 60–65 percent of national income, versus 50–55 percent in Brazil, 45–50 percent in the US, and 30–35 percent in Europe. Even worse: the vast gap between the top 10 percent (who remain overwhelmingly white) and the bottom 90 percent has widened further since the end of apartheid. This sad fact is partly explained by international factors, such as deregulation and the explosion of incomes from finance (a very important sector in South Africa), the rise in commodity prices (which chiefly benefits a narrow white minority), and endemic tax and social dumping. But it's also explained by the shortcomings of the ANC's policies. Public schools and services in the most disadvantaged areas are still mediocre. No ambitious land reform has been carried out, in a country where blacks were denied the right to own land and confined in townships and reservations from 1913, under the Natives Land Act, until 1990. Land, real estate, and financial wealth remain largely in the hands of the white elite, along with mineral and natural resources. The timid measures of Black Economic Empowerment (BEE), which aimed to require white shareholders to hand over a fraction of their shares to blacks, on the basis of voluntary transactions at the market price, have benefited only a tiny minority of blacks who already had the means – or the political connections – to buy them.

The result is predictable: the ANC is increasingly challenged from its left by the Economic Freedom Fighters party, which proposes a series of radical measures, such as education and social security for all, land redistribution, and nationalization of mineral resources. The white minority (14 percent of the population in 1990, only 9 percent today) is panicking; last week, a white deputy, a sort of local version of France's right-wing populist Nadine Morano, called for the return of the last apartheid president. To retake the initiative, the ANC could try to put in place a national minimum wage starting in 2016, and use it as a tool to reduce inequality, as President Lula did in Brazil. Some also envision the establishment of a progressive tax on capital, to gradually redistribute economic power. Such a plan was on the table between 1994 and 1999 before finally being abandoned by the ANC. According to former president Thabo Mbeki, the police and army, then still led by whites, wouldn't have allowed it.

One thing is certain: whether it's a question of nationalizing mines or simply any plan to tax multinationals and wealth holders more significantly, South Africa would need cooperation from the rich countries rather than our current hypocrisy. South Africa's financial elite freely admits this. In the 1980s, they were forced to negotiate, but now they can easily transfer their money abroad and to tax havens. Indeed, international financial opacity is a genuine scourge for Africa: an estimated 30 to 50 percent of the continent's financial assets are held in tax havens (versus 10 percent for Europe). All Europe and the U.S. need to do is decide, for instance in the framework of the transatlantic treaty under negotiation, and it would be technically easy to put in place a genuine world register of financial assets. As Gabriel Zucman explains in *The Hidden Wealth of Nations*, the authorities would only need to come together and take control of the private securities custodians which currently fulfill this function (Clearstream and Eurostream in Europe, Depository Trust Corporation in the U.S.). Africa doesn't need aid; it simply needs an international legal system that can protect it from permanent pillage.

During the night of November 13, 2015, ISIL-trained militants launched a series of coordinated attacks against civilians in Paris that left 130 dead. In France and throughout the West, government leaders weighed the merits of military retaliation.

A Crackdown Alone Will Solve Nothing

Le Monde, November 21, 2015

Part of the response to terrorism must be security-based. A strike against Daesh is needed; those who belong to it must be stopped. But we also have to think about the political context of the violence, about the humiliations and injustices that allow this movement to enjoy significant support in the Middle East and call forth bloody actions in Europe. Ultimately the real stakes are about creating an equitable model of social development, over there and over here.

There's no question: terrorism is fueled by the inegalitarian powder keg of the Middle East, which we largely helped to create. Daesh, 'the Islamic State in Iraq and the Levant,' is a direct product of the disintegration of the Iraqi regime, and more generally the collapse of the system of regional borders established in 1920.

After Iraq's annexation of Kuwait in 1990–91, the united great powers sent their troops to restore the oil to the emirs – and to Western companies. Meanwhile, a new cycle of asymmetric and technological wars was launched – a few

hundred dead in the coalition to 'liberate' Kuwait versus tens
of thousands on the Iraqi side. This logic was pushed to its
limit in the second Iraq War, between 2003 and 2011: roughly
500,000 Iraqi dead versus 4,000 American soldiers killed, all
to avenge the 3,000 who died on September 11, though that
had nothing to do with Iraq. Today this reality, amplified by
the Israeli-Palestinian conflict, with its extreme asymmetry
of human costs and its lack of a political horizon, serves as
justification for every atrocity perpetrated by the jihadists.
Let's hope that France and Russia, on the move since the
American fiasco, do less damage and bring forth fewer bloody
actions.

Concentration of resources

Beyond the clash of religions, the concentration of oil
resources within small, unpopulated territories shapes and
undermines the region's whole political and social system.
Looking at the zone that stretches from Egypt to Iran, and
running through Syria, Iraq, and the Arabian Peninsula, a
population of 300 million, we find that the oil monarchies
hold a combined 60 to 70 percent of regional GDP, for barely
10 percent of the population, which makes the region the
most unequal on the planet.

It must be made clear that a minority of the population in
the oil kingdoms appropriate a disproportionate share of this
bounty, while large groups (women and immigrant workers,
especially) are kept in semi-slavery. And it's these regimes
that are militarily and politically supported by the Western
powers, which are only too happy to get back a few crumbs
to finance their football teams or through weapons sales. It's

not surprising that our sermons on democracy and social justice count for little among the youth of the Middle East.

To gain credibility, we must show these populations that we care more about the region's social development and political integration than about our financial interests and relationships with the ruling families.

Denial of democracy

In concrete terms, oil money must go to regional development first. The Egyptian authorities' total budget to fund the entire educational system of a country of nearly 90 million is less than $10 billion (€9.4 billion) in 2015. A few hundred kilometers away, oil income reaches $300 billion for Saudi Arabia and its 30 million inhabitants, and it exceeds $100 billion for Qatar and its 300,000 Qataris. A development model that is so unequal can only lead to disaster. To sanction it is criminal.

As for the lofty rhetoric about democracy and elections, we have to stop deploying it only when it suits us. In 2012, in Egypt, Mohamed Morsi was elected president in an honest election, hardly a trivial event in Arab electoral history. By 2013, he'd been ousted by the generals, who swiftly executed thousands of Muslim Brotherhood members even though their voluntary activities have often helped to compensate for the shortcomings of the Egyptian state. A few months later, France wiped the slate clean to sell Egypt warships and thereby grasp a share of the country's meager public resources. Let us hope this denial of democracy won't have the same deadly consequences as did the Algerian military's civil war – sparking obstruction of a democratically elected Islamist party in 1992.

The question remains: How could young people raised in France conflate Baghdad and the Paris *banlieue*, seeking to import here the conflicts taking place over there? Nothing can excuse this bloody, macho, pathetic atrocity. We may simply note that unemployment and job discrimination (which is particularly intense for those who've checked off all the right boxes in terms of education, experience, etc., as recent studies have shown) can't be helping. Europe, which before the recession managed to accommodate a net immigration flow of one million people annually, with falling unemployment, must relaunch its model of job creation and social integration. Austerity is what led to the rise of national selfishness and tensions around national identity. Social development with equity is how hatred will be defeated.

Index